The Inclusive classroom

a practical guide for educators

SiriNam S. Khalsa

Illustrated by Yoshi Miyake

Good Year Books

An Imprint of Addison-Wesley Educational Publishers, Inc.

Good Year Books are available for most basic curriculum subjects plus many enrichment areas. For more Good Year Books, contact your local bookseller or educational dealer. For a complete catalog with information about other Good Year Books, please write to:

Good Year Books
1900 East Lake Avenue
Glenview, Illinois 60025

Design: Double Click Printing and Graphics, Inc.

ISBN 0-673-58646-4

1 2 3 4 5 6 7 8 9 -ML- 06 05 04 03 02 01 00 99 98

Dedication

This book is sincerely dedicated to all our children which include the many students I have had the privilege to teach in public schools, educational collaboratives, and summer camps. They all have and continue to inspire me to keep learning, growing, and developing as a teacher. Thank you.

Acknowledgments

This book evolved from a realization that the direction public school education has taken requires that all teachers need the skills and understanding of how to reach and teach all children in the mainstream classroom. As the material presented in this book developed, I was constantly rewarded by the pleasure of working with many individuals who are trying to meet this challenge set before us.

I wish to thank the following individuals for their support and influence. Thank you to those administrators, teachers, and counselors from Kennedy Middle School and the Springfield MA School District who are helping to achieve the goals of the inclusive classroom. Special thanks to an inspiring principal, Mrs. Veta Daley, for her leadership and support of the learning needs of all students. Thanks to Laura Strom and the editorial staff at Good Year Books. Appreciation to John Ryan for his early inspiration. And a heartfelt thank you to my wife Kirn Kaur, and family for their never-ending love and support.

Table of Contents

Table of Contents

INTRODUCTION
DEFINING INCLUSION

Inclusive education has arrived. The benefits of including students with special needs in age-appropriate regular education classes in neighborhood schools are making true believers out of parents, teachers, administrators, and students. I've been fortunate, for the past few years, to be part of a school system that has worked hard to make the inclusion process a success for all involved. However, I also have seen the need to give teachers more practical information so that they can develop strategies and environments to support inclusive classrooms.

A few years ago I realized that many parents, teachers, and students with disabilities were requesting more educational options. The walls of segregated classrooms started to fall down and the roles and responsibilities of all educators began to change. Initially, as a special educator, I was resistant to support a philosophy that I believed could be detrimental to the self-esteem of students with learning difficulties. I also didn't think I had enough time to investigate the possibilities inherent in inclusive classrooms, and I wasn't excited about having to team teach. In other words, I was content with the status quo.

After visiting a school where inclusion was being successfully implemented using a co-teaching model, however, my interest was piqued. I began attending conferences and listening to colleagues talk about the possible benefits of providing instructional and emotional support to children with disabilities in the regular classroom setting. I also discovered ways to assist teachers in these efforts with new ideas for instructional modifications.

Even though some school districts are very supportive of full- and part-time inclusive classrooms, it isn't always an easy journey for all involved. Classroom teachers may express concerns about not being competent enough or trained to deal with children

with disabilities. Not only are we bringing children with special needs into the regular classroom, but all teachers, regardless of their training, are now expected to serve all students regardless of their individual needs! The majority of teachers intrinsically appreciate that this is a positive direction for children and adults to take, but that does not make it any less challenging. Through my experiences with inclusive classrooms, I now realize that inclusion is like a mirror that reflects positively on all those who embrace it.

What Is Inclusion?

The American Heritage Dictionary defines *inclusion* as "the act of including or belonging together from beginning to end."

Inclusion is the natural process of living in a democratic society. Feeling part of and involved in our families, local communities, country, and humanity is the foundation of the life we lead. Unfortunately, for many years we have excluded children with disabilities from fully participating in the general school setting. Children with special needs have been sent to private schools, collaboratives, separate classrooms, or traditional pull-out programs. Inclusive education is eliminating segregation of children who learn differently and is changing our perception about what we as educators can do to set the tone for acceptance.

Presently, inclusive education programs are being implemented across the nation in large and small urban, suburban, and rural districts. Many factors have influenced the movement of regular and special education toward closer cooperation. These factors include: federal legislation (PL 94–142), student self-advocacy, and parental support for both access and equality in school programs for all children. In addition, there is growing concern about the economic implications of setting up substantially separate programs for students with disabilities. These factors have also helped educators realize that the traditional way of dividing students into two classifications, normal and special, is now neither realistic nor productive.

What Are Some of the Qualities That Define Inclusive Classrooms?

- Students previously served by special education classrooms now being served in the general classroom setting for all or part of the day

- Special and regular education teachers working together as a team in the same classroom

- Special education and regular education staff planning lessons together

- All staff working together in designing a classroom to accentuate the success of all its members

- Regular classroom teachers being given relevant information on students with special needs in order to assist them in adapting or modifying classroom instruction, assessment, and behavioral management

The Illusion of Inclusion

It is equally important to understand what inclusion is not.

- "Dumping" students with special needs in regular classrooms without necessary supports and services

- Trading off instructional quality for inclusion goals

- Cutting back or eliminating needed special education services

- Expecting all students to learn at the same time, at the same pace, and in the same way

- Requiring regular education teachers to teach all students without the support needed to succeed

- Sacrificing the quality education of general needs students

Inclusion begins with the decision to educate as many students as possible in the regular classroom setting in their own neighborhood schools. *Neighborhood school* is defined as "the school the child would be attending if he or she were not disabled."

Inclusion of special students in the general classroom is an ongoing process. This process may look different for each school, each teacher, and each student. However, there are some consistent qualities as well as practices that are interwoven within each classroom. Qualities such as **cooperation, communication**, and **commitment** to the inclusive process are essential for success.

Each unique situation should also have the flexibility to develop and make needed changes from year to year, month to month, week to week, and in some situations, day to day. Today as more and more schools adopt inclusion, an increasing number of teachers are finding it difficult to understand "how to make it work." It's important to begin to understand the different options available to you and your school, to make inclusion work for all students.

Each student's academic and social needs will determine the model option necessary for meeting those needs. The student also may be involved with a combination of model options throughout the school day. Facilitating a school environment that cultivates an openness around different model options, as well as acceptance for children with diverse learning needs, is an important first step. The successful inclusion program will encourage schools to create programs around children's academic, social, and behavioral needs rather than attempting to fit all students into existing programs.

When determining which model option is most appropriate for a student's special needs, both regular and special education faculty need to work together in a unified manner in order to promote favorable inclusion environments.

> *"All great minds DON'T think alike"*

What Does an Inclusive School Look Like?

Working toward specific educational goals for the included child will set a tone that supports shared responsibility, accountability, and concern for all children. Following are some characteristics of teams and schools that enhance collaboration:

- Shared ownership of the responsibility to educate all children by general and special educators

- A continuum of classroom model options

- A variety of teaching models, focusing on the possible advantages of each one

- Flexibility and openness to different teaching as well as behavioral management strategies

- Shared goals and beliefs pertaining to the appropriate curriculum adaptations and modifications possibly needed for the success of the included child

- Shared awareness of all students' abilities as well as disabilities—*All great minds don't think alike.*

What Are the Classroom Model Options?

- **Full Inclusion Model**—The student participates all day in a regular classroom with age-appropriate peers. The special education staff co-teaches with the regular education teacher or provides consultative support.

- **Mainstreaming Model**—This was one of the first terms used to describe the education of students with special needs within regular classrooms. The student takes part in activities in the regular class based on his or her acceptable level of performance and behavior.

- **Social Mainstreaming Model**—The student is included in the regular classroom for the main purpose of providing him or her with appropriate interactions with nondisabled students. The student can be given modified or parallel assignments, but is not required to complete instructional assignments.

- **Pull-Out (Resource Room) Model**—Special education staff provides academic support to one or more students outside the classroom, as needed.

- **Nonacademic Model**—The student participates in regular classes in the areas of physical education, music, and art.

- **Self-Contained Model**—The student remains in a special education classroom or resource room for all or part of the school day.

These terms represent many classroom model options considered appropriate for meeting the needs of students with special needs. It's important to remember that inclusion involves multiple model options. Other model options that are developed through the collaboration of faculty, parents, and administrators can only add to the flexibility necessary to support all children's ability to learn.

This Book As a Tool for Teachers

Teachers need tools, or resources, to build successful programs in which all children have the opportunity for meaningful, educational experiences regardless of learning styles and ability. The purpose of this book is to share practical guidance with you as you work toward achieving the often arduous but ultimately rewarding task of creating and running inclusive schools. As you strive to create learning environments where all children can experience success, develop lifelong friendships, and gain skills that enable them to become contributing members of society, you will also realize the need for practical strategies to support your goals.

> *"Inclusion is not an end in itself.*
> *It is a means to an end, and that end is*
> *improved learning for every student."*

The Inclusive Classroom offers educators, parents, administrators, and other school personnel in the elementary and lower middle-school grades a basic understanding of what is involved in making inclusion work. This book will provide basic techniques to increase successful opportunities for the children being included in your classrooms. In Chapter 1 there is an explanation of the types of disabilities and other factors determining achievement, reasons for trying inclusion, and factors in determining whether inclusion is appropriate. In Chapter 2 you will find the most recent research on how to address students' different learning styles and multiple intelligences in the classroom. In Chapter 3, you will find teaching tools such as easy-to-use activities, staff communication forms, and effective behavioral management strategies for immediate implementation. Chapter 4 is dedicated to curriculum modification strategies and lesson designs that will assist all students in reaching your teaching goals. Included in Chapter 5 is a curriculum entitled "How to Succeed in Eight Lessons," which has been found successful in aiding children in learning how to learn. In Chapter 6 you will learn how to manage classroom behaviors successfully. Chapter 7 gives strategies for dealing with ten specific negative behavior types. Chapter 8 discusses how to develop a partnership with parents and how parents can help. The Appendix contains references and a list of organizations you can join to provide additional support.

Throughout this book, you will see how your school community can effectively work together in helping all children reach their learning potential. This may include children with learning disabilities; physical, social, and emotional problems; attention deficit disorders; and speech and language needs, as well as those who are underachieving for a variety of other factors. It is my belief, as well as experience, that most children with mild to moderate disabilities can have a successful educational experience in the mainstream of our school system. I also firmly believe that success cannot be achieved without two things in place:

1. A shared mindset that understands inclusion is a challenging proposition and one that no one is going to attempt if they do not truly believe that it is possible and necessary

2. A commitment to creating a collaborative partnership with all who are involved in the inclusion process

It's important to clarify one point in regard to teaching "all children in inclusive classrooms." This book was written with understanding and genuine respect for all teachers, parents, and students who are involved in the inclusion process. It was also written with the awareness that the regular classroom setting may not always be the best or least restrictive learning environment for every student. Every child is entitled to an appropriate placement that will offer him or her the most effective educational opportunity consistent with his or her needs.

Inclusion is not an end in itself. It is a means to an end, and that end is improved learning for every student. *The Inclusive Classroom* was written to enable all educators who are participating in the challenging and exciting process of inclusion to build a solid foundation for success.

CHAPTER 1
GETTING STARTED

Diversity comes in many shapes, sizes, and forms. The inclusive classroom welcomes diversity and the wide range of student needs that accompany students' differences. Teachers who help children understand and discuss differences help create an educational environment that supports empathy for all individuals.

Educators and administrators understand that our laws require us to sometimes define children before we can serve them through special education programs. By definition, students with special needs are in need of and entitled to special approaches to learning from our schools. Special and general education teachers are being asked to meet the learning needs of all students who enter their classrooms. Categorizing can add some clarity in determining what type of instruction is needed for the student with learning problems. For example, because the type of instruction needed depends upon the nature of the difficulty, it's important to distinguish between children who have a learning disability and those who are educationally delayed. The child who is educationally delayed because of mental retardation, emotional disturbance, deafness, and so forth, may need a different kind of instructional approach than a child with learning disabilities. The special educator is trained to assist the regular classroom teacher with these distinctions.

To help teachers understand the differences in these classifications for instructional purposes, brief descriptions of the special needs categories follow.

Defining Types of Disabilities

Learning Disabilities

Children with learning disabilities require a different method of instruction to learn what is taught in class. For this reason some people refer to learning disabled (LD) as meaning "learning different." Students with learning disabilities compose the largest, approximately 50 percent, and often the most misunderstood group of children receiving special education services. Children with LD are not less intelligent than most of their peers, yet they often need alternative learning strategies to experience success in school. Some of our greatest achievers, such as Albert Einstein, had a learning disability.

Some children with LD exhibit poor motor coordination and body image. These students are easily spotted in gym class, since they usually perform poorly in physical education activities for their age level. If this is the case, modified exercises and activities may be needed to help students with disabilities take advantage of the same physical, emotional, and social benefits of exercise, recreation, and leisure activities that other students enjoy. Many children with LD could learn more easily if taught how to better organize their materials and assignments and if given extra support in this area. Some simple and effective ways to help students get organized are described in "How to Succeed in Eight Lessons," Chapter 5.

> *"Some of our greatest achievers, such as Albert Einstein, had a learning disability."*

Mental Retardation

A child who is identified as having mental retardation has difficulty in learning how to read, write, spell, or calculate at his or her age level. Presently, the degree of mental retardation is determined by the child's IQ. It is known that a child whose IQ is 50, 60, or 70 has a mental level of 3 to 4 years at the age of 6. This means that the child possibly will be 9 to 12 years old before he or she has the prerequisite skills for reading. Mental retardation is not a disease, nor should it be confused with mental illness. Children with mental retardation grow into adults with mental retardation; they do not remain "eternal children." All individuals who are mentally disabled have the capacity to learn, develop, and grow. The great majority can become economically productive, fully participating members of society. The student's education should be general, practical, and adapted to the slower rate of development.

Mental retardation can be caused by any condition that impairs development of the brain before and during birth or in the childhood years. Some of the most common causes

include genetic irregularities; drug and/or alcohol abuse; problems before, during, or after birth; and environmental factors that, according to the President's Committee on Mental Retardation (1985), account for 75 percent of our nation's citizens with mental retardation.

Some children will use the term "retarded" to tease a peer who did something wrong. The teacher can use this as a learning opportunity to help children understand the implications of using this term, and the difference between having a mental disability and doing something annoying or inappropriate.

Speech and Sensory Handicaps

This category includes visual, speech, and hearing impairments that affect the ability to learn. Deaf children, for example, are often delayed in reading because deafness interferes with the development of language. Children with speech difficulties have problems with pronunciation and speech fluency. Children with language disorders demonstrate difficulties in the use of language. Speech and language pathologists have developed ways to assess language disorders and teach those who have them. These children often need additional time to express themselves in class. A simple technique to facilitate verbal responses with this type of student is to offer him or her a choice of answers: "Is Boston a city or a state?"

Emotional Disturbance and Behavioral Disorders

Students exhibiting an emotional disability are often delayed educationally as well. These children may demonstrate a variety of behavioral problems that may have existed for a long time across a range of environmental settings. Some of these behavioral problems include verbal aggression, confrontational behavior, impulsive and uninhibited behavior, resistance to change, and frustration, even when confronted with a simple task.

Certain behaviors, however, should be targeted as priorities in the inclusive classroom when working with children who have an emotional disturbance. These target behaviors include:

- Excessive absences or tardiness

- Defiance of authority

- Erratic and explosive outbursts

- Poor social relationships

- Poor attention span

- Low frustration level

- Inability to remain seated for a short period of time

Students who exhibit emotional and behavioral problems are often the most difficult to work with. For this reason, Chapter 6 is dedicated to managing behavior problems in the classroom. Possible causes and instructional considerations are provided. Many children who fall into this emotional and behavioral category are being identified today as having an Attention Deficit/Hyperactivity Disorder (ADHD). This is diagnosed by clinical assessment and includes information from all those who know the child. (See Chapter 6, Managing Behaviors in an Inclusive Classroom.)

Physical Disabilities

Children with a physical disability have difficulty using their bodies. The cause of their disabilities may be cerebral palsy, muscular dystrophy, spina bifida, or multiple sclerosis. Children with severe physical disabilities may receive services in motor development from specialists, such as occupational or physical therapists. Many children with physical disabilities are of normal intelligence, and thus should not be prevented from participating in class activities. The child in a wheelchair, just as one who brings an inhaler for chronic asthma to class, should be expected to participate as fully as possible.

Other Factors Determining Achievement

There are other factors resulting in children not achieving in school. The following are three of the most prevalent external reasons for underachieving. These children aren't necessarily receiving special educational services.

Lack of Opportunity

This refers to a child who has matured at a normal rate emotionally, socially, and linguistically, but who is behind academically. Although there is a difference

between the student's potential and achievement, the student is not considered learning disabled. Take, for example, a 9-year-old child who has moved several times during the past two years and who is consequently lacking continuity in his or her schooling. This child will "catch up" if given consistent developmental reading and arithmetic tutoring, beginning at his or her level of competence.

Economic and Cultural Disadvantage

Some children underachieve in school due to a lack of support from their home environments. They, therefore, develop a resistance toward learning as a result of low self-concept and a lack of positive role models and encouragement. Notable early education compensatory programs for at-risk pre-schoolers exist, such as Head Start and Parent and Child Centers.

Why Try Inclusion?

Many children across the country live in communities in which exposure to people with any kind of difference is limited. Interaction with children with disabilities at school can change how they view individual differences.

Why then should children with special needs be educated in regular classrooms? We have identified the types of students who would most likely participate in an inclusive program. But what are the possible benefits for children who participate in an inclusive classroom?

Benefits for Students

- Interaction with regular education peers
- Increased social skills
- Labeling is de-emphasized
- Higher expectations for learning
- Increased sense of school community
- Increased real-world learning
- Opportunity for peers to see that the differences in students with special needs are superficial

Benefits for Teachers

- Increased collegiality among special and regular education faculty
- Shared resources
- Special educators able to serve more students
- Teachers increase their instructional skills repertoire

When Is Inclusion Appropriate?

Before deciding when inclusion is appropriate, one must answer questions concerning the following four factors.

1. **The student:** What are his or her academic and social needs? What is the severity of the disability? What is his or her learning style? How adaptable is the student?

2. **The teacher:** How receptive is he or she to inclusion? What skills does he or she possess? Has the teacher been prepared to have students with disabilities enter his or her classroom? Is there adequate staffing? Is the teacher willing to create an environment that supports diversity in learning styles?

3. **The class makeup:** How resistant or accepting are the students? What percentage of students exhibit emotional immaturity when it comes to bullying, teasing, and making fun of others? Are there appropriate role models in the class? Are cooperative learning activities already being implemented?

4. **The parent:** Parents want the best educational program for their child. Inclusion isn't always the best option. Discussion surrounding inclusive and noninclusive steps that meet the student's academic, social/emotional, and behavioral goals need to take place. Communication between teacher and parent is an essential step.

These four factors can act as a guide toward more informed discussions about integrating of children with special needs. With cooperative planning and an understanding of the student's needs, a solid foundation for successful inclusion can be built.

Beliefs That Support Teaching In an Inclusive School

LIBERATE LEARNING	OR	*LIMIT* LEARNING
All children are capable of high achievement, not just the fastest or most confident children.	VS.	Only the few bright children can achieve at high level.
Consistent effort and effective strategies are the ingredients for success.	VS.	Inborn intelligence is the determinant of success.
You are not supposed to understand everything the first time around.	VS.	Speed is what counts. Faster is smarter.
Mistakes help one learn.	VS.	Mistakes are a sign of mental weakness.
Successful students work together and solicit help from one another.	VS.	Competition is necessary to bring out the best in children . . . or . . . good students can do it on their own.

As an educator, which column reflects your belief system?

Redefined Job Responsibilities in an Inclusive Classroom

TITLE	TRADITIONAL RESPONSIBILITIES	REDEFINED RESPONSIBILITIES
Teacher	Students who do not "fit" into the mainstream class due to academic or disabilities are referred for diagnosis, remediation, and possible removal to a separate setting. Teaches all children in the same way, and at the same time.	Works with the special educators and other support staff as a team for teaching and reaching all children in the mainstream classroom. Collaboratively plans and teaches with other educators to meet the learning styles and needs of all children. Uses cooperative learning strategies to encourage peer support for one another.
Special Educator	Teaches students with special needs in resource rooms, self-contained classrooms, and special schools.	Collaborates with general education staff and other support personnel to meet the academic and social needs of all learners. Team teaches with general educators.

Diversity Acceptance Checklist

My Attitude Toward Acceptance . . .

Accepting diversity in your classroom begins with being aware of your values, thoughts, and behaviors. Accepting diverse learning styles in your students will help create a learning environment that will erase labels and focus on individual talents as well as group cohesiveness. Ask yourself these questions and let them act as a guide as you check your attitude toward acceptance:

1. Do I see a student with special needs as an individual with disabilities or a disabled individual?

2. Do I try to support individual capabilities and adapt to students needs?

3. Am I comfortable interacting with students with mental and physical disabilities?

4. Do I assist students in communicating their thoughts and feelings in alternative ways (e.g., drawing, sign language, communication board, etc.)?

5. Do I attempt to determine students' diverse learning styles and teach with them in mind?

6. Do I use a variety of instructional strategies that encourage group work (e.g., cooperative groups, learning buddies, peer reading, etc.)?

7. Do I understand where, when, and how to offer support to a student with special needs?

8. Do I know where to start in the process of choosing appropriate adaptations and modifications to classroom activities, curriculum, and materials?

9. Is my classroom set up to be responsive to a variety of instructional and behavioral needs?

10. Do I adjust the physical arrangement of the room for students with disabilities?

11. Do I try to use a variety of assessment procedures for all students (e.g., oral testing, contract grading, point systems, pass/fail, etc.)?

12. Do I set up student conferences to provide one-to-one feedback?

13. Do I view students with special needs as "my" students?

14. Do I use encouragement more than reprimands?

15. Do I use alternative approaches toward behavioral management (e.g., active listening, planned ignoring, time-out, check lists, etc.)?

16. Do I feel comfortable communicating with parents of students with special needs?

17. Am I comfortable with support services provided in my classroom?

18. Am I comfortable with team collaboration (co-teaching, co-planning, etc.)?

19. Do I see my responsibility as a "teacher" as one who facilitates the learning process of all students who enter my classroom?

20. Do I trust the administration to give me adequate support?

My personal action plan for growth:

_____

_____

_____

_____

_____

_____

_____

_____

_____

_____

_____

_____

_____

_____

_____

_____

_____

_____

_____

CHAPTER 2
LEARNING STYLES AND MULTIPLE INTELLIGENCES— HOW CHILDREN LEARN

All children do not learn in the same way. There is an increasing amount of information based on how children learn and the different styles or modalities that facilitate the learning process. Special educators are trained to approach teaching in a variety of different ways to ensure that students with learning difficulties process the information being taught. Teaching strategies that include role-play, group discussion, visual aids, and hands-on activities are not necessarily new to the special educator. All teachers are now being exposed to the recent literature that addresses the importance of understanding how "learning styles" affect the way all children think, behave, approach learning, and process information. It is important that all children understand that uniqueness not only encompasses our likes and dislikes, culture, gender, and race, but also includes the way we learn.

I recommend to teachers that they share this important information with their students during the beginning weeks of school. This can be communicated to students in a very neutral and matter-of-fact manner such as, "Each of us is unique in that we learn in many different ways. To help all of you succeed, I will probably treat each one of you a little differently throughout the year and include a variety of ways of teaching you in class."

"A student's style of learning refers to the student's general behavior, attitude, and temperament when presented with a learning task. The learning styles in an academic situation influence the effectiveness of learning. The learning style of the student may be at odds with the style required to succeed in a traditional education system. Analysis of the student's learning style can provide insight into the nature of the learning difficulties."

(Carbo, M.; R. Dunn; and K. Dunn. *Teaching Students to Read Through Their Individual Learning Styles.* Reston Publishing Company, 1986.)

Five Learning Modalities and Teaching Strategies The following
descriptions are of basic learning modalities and some suggested teaching strategies that can be used to support a student's preferred style of learning. It's important to understand that a student's strength might be in one of these areas, or in several. When two or more areas are equally efficient, the result is mixed, or multi-modality, strengths. Children with multi-modality strengths seem to have a learning advantage in the

classroom. They are better able to process the information being taught regardless of its presentation. There are a number of checklists that can assist teachers in gathering information on students' learning modalities, several are included in the Appendix under "Recommended Resources."

Visual Learners: Students whose preference is the visual channel learn best by looking, seeing, observing, watching, and visualizing. Research has shown that approximately 30 percent of elementary school-aged children are visual learners. To support these students, you can use these teaching strategies:

Visual Learner Teaching Strategies

- Supplement lectures with visual aids such as: color transparencies, maps, charts, graphs, filmstrips, and videos.

- Write information on the chalkboard as well as give it verbally. Provide a written copy of board work if needed. The use of graphs, pictures, key words, and important facts also should accompany verbal directions and presentations. Give a copy of assignments in written form, weekly or daily.

- Include the use of graphic organizers such as webs, outlines, and charts when giving instructions to assist visual learners in comprehending assignments.

- Provide books with illustrations that accompany text.

- Use colored flashcards as well as colored indicators on rulers and yardsticks, and highlight important passages in their texts.

- Use word searches, word cards to arrange in sentences, letter cards to spell words, word games such as Scrabble®, and crossword puzzles to assist in reading skills.

- Allow students to give written reports or projects as well as oral ones.

- Have students observe experiments, demonstrations, animal behavior, and role-play.

- Use mnemonic devices and associations to aid memory (e.g., Italy is the shape of a boot.).

Auditory Learners: These students make up approximately 25 percent of elementary school-aged children. They learn by listening to others and themselves. It's important to emphasize the difference between "hearing" and "listening" by playing direction-following games such as Simon Says. Having auditory learners repeat oral instructions will reinforce comprehension. To support auditory learners you can include these teaching strategies:

Auditory Learner Teaching Strategies

- Tape textbook material for students to listen to while reading.

- Give verbal as well as written directions. You can tape-record your instructions or lecture and then play the tape back to the class or individual while they begin the assignment.

- Involve students in small- and large-group discussions; learning partners read important information (and do oral activities prior to independent/silent work).

- Give an oral rather than written test. For inclusive students, allow tests to be administered by special education staff in the resource room.

- Use phonetic approaches for reading and decoding skills.

- Use word games, spelling bees, audio tapes, and rhyming melodies to reinforce learning.

- Have students interact/verbalize through brainstorming, panels, partner work, and interviews.

Kinesthetic or Tactile Learners: Approximately 15 percent of elementary school-aged children are kinesthetically oriented. The remaining 30 percent of children have a mixed or multi-modality strength. Kinesthetic learners learn by moving, touching, and directly experiencing through hands-on activities. These students need to use manipulatives to activate their ability to process information. They are usually very energetic children who have difficulty sitting for a long period of time. Their energy needs to be directed through activities that require them to translate verbal instruction into bodily kinesthetic expression. For example, in a vocabulary lesson about prefixes, one child is the prefix "un" and another is the root word "like." They stand next to each other to make the word "unlike" and apart to demonstrate how the prefix changes the meaning of the root word. The range of topics is endless. To support kinesthetic learners, you can use the following:

Kinesthetic Learner Teaching Strategies

- Use role-play and simulations to reinforce lesson.

- Allow students to use body movements to demonstrate teaching concepts such as raising arms to demonstrate a right angle, horizontal and vertical lines, or the x- and y-axis of a graph.

- Allow students to build models, draw pictures, make bulletin boards, design collages, and so on. (You may want to have a piece of clay or spongy ball ready for the tactile student to hold when they're expected to sit and pay attention. They're usually so grateful for the opportunity to touch and manipulate something that they return the object without a problem.)

- Let students move about, for example, to another seating area during class or to deliver something to another teacher in the building.

Impulsive Learners: This type of learner responds very quickly to a given problem with very little consideration to the possible outcomes. Students with learning disabilities often respond in an impulsive manner that is usually detrimental to their school performance. These students need guidance and practice in approaching their work with more deliberation, considering alternatives before choosing a response to a problem. To promote a more reflective approach to their schoolwork, employ self-monitoring strategies using high-interest materials to promote active involvement in the learning process (e.g., stopping after each paragraph and asking, "What did I just read?").

Active Versus Passive Learners: Successful experiences in learning require an active or involved dynamic in the learning process. Students who are active learners use many effective thinking strategies (e.g., organization and self-questioning) that promote their involvement in the work and increase their motivation to learn.

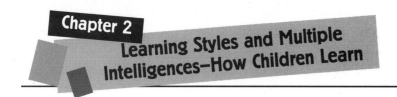

From *The Inclusive Classroom.* Copyright © 1999 Good Year Books.

On the other hand, students who lack the interest, skills, and/or self-concept to be active in the learning process will usually approach the learning task in a passive manner. Consequently, they become frustrated and uninvolved. These students need encouragement and small successes to build up their confidence.

In summary, knowing the learning styles of your students will help you develop cognitive empathy, or a way of getting into your students' heads. Learning styles help us to identify the comfort zones of our students, but should not act as an excuse for them not to participate in class. Teaching to different learning styles will enhance your ability to effectively teach all students.

> *"Teaching to different learning styles will enhance your ability to effectively teach all students."*

Creating a Responsive Classroom Environment

Creating a classroom environment responsive to the learning styles of your students is oftentimes a challenge. Classroom space is scarce in many of our overcrowded schools. Due to space restrictions, it is often difficult to be creative with seating arrangements and learning centers. Nevertheless, it's important to evaluate how you set up your classroom and its effect on the students' ability to learn. Students sitting in neat rows of desks facing the front of the room, where a teacher either sits or lectures from, is one way to organize a classroom, but by no means the only or best way.

Arranging a classroom environment that supports the different learning styles of all students takes some brainstorming, but the results are worth it. The effects of a well-planned classroom area will undoubtedly show as students' participation and cooperation increases.

The following questions serve as guidelines for arranging a responsive classroom environment.

Checklist for Creating a Responsive Classroom Environment

✔ Are there clearly defined interest and storage areas for materials that are easily accessible to students?

✔ Is the room attractive to the eye (displays of selected pictures or materials that relate to children's interests or class studies, plants on windowsills, etc.)?

✔ Are students taught how to display work and how to label and describe this work?

✔ How is the furniture arranged? Does furniture (shelves, desks, tables, bulletin boards) throughout the entire room create defined work areas that are appropriate to the age and development of the children?

✔ Are there active and quiet areas as well as a carpeted area for informal learning?

✔ Is the furniture arranged so you can see the entire room from any part of the room?

✔ Can you move around the room without feeling crowded?

✔ Is there a meeting area (in elementary grades) large enough for the whole class to sit in a circle and that can be used at any time of the day?

✔ Is material rotated on shelves and in interest areas to reflect and enhance themes of study to keep students interested and challenged?

✔ Are there centers for group and individual learning?

The classroom environment provides much of the clarity, comfort, and structure needed for students to be actively engaged in the learning process. Many teachers are incorporating learning centers in their classrooms to expand the opportunities for reaching a variety of learning needs.

It is highly recommended that you involve your students in the process of experimenting with different arrangements to determine what works best for your classroom.

From *The Inclusive Classroom*. Copyright © 1999 Good Year Books.

"Almost eighty years after the first intelligence tests (IQ tests) were developed, a Harvard psychologist named Howard Gardner challenged this commonly held belief. Saying that our culture had defined intelligence too narrowly, he proposed in the book Frames of Mind *(Gardner 1983) the existence of at least seven intelligences. In this theory of multiple intelligences (MI theory), Gardner sought to broaden the scope of human potential beyond the confines of the IQ score. Gardner suggested that intelligence has more to do with the capacity for (1) solving problems and (2) fashioning products in a context-rich and naturalistic setting."*

(Armstrong, Thomas. "Multiple Intelligences in the Classroom," *Association for Supervision and Curriculum Development*, 1994.)

Seven Types of Intelligences

Linguistic Intelligence "Word Smart": These people are very good at using their verbal and language skills and are often storytellers, journalists, poets, editors, playwrights, or politicians. Linguistic learners enjoy word games like Scrabble®, anagrams, Password®, and crossword puzzles. These children usually have a good vocabulary for their age and excel in reading, spelling, and verbal communication.

Logical-Mathematical Intelligence "Number Smart": These individuals have a natural talent for using numbers effectively (e.g., as a mathematician or tax accountant) and are able to reason well (e.g., as a scientist or computer programmer). These learners are adept in problem solving, calculation, inference, and hypothesis testing. These learners enjoy playing chess, checkers, or other strategy games (in preschool, board games requiring counting squares).

Spatial Intelligence "Art Smart": These learners have a talent in perceiving the visual-spatial world accurately (e.g., as a scout), and to re-create that world they see so clearly (e.g., as an artist, interior decorator, architect, or inventor). These children enjoy art activities, puzzles, mazes, Where's Waldo?®, or other similar activities. They get more out of pictures than words while reading and are usually found doodling on workbooks, worksheets, and other materials.

Bodily-Kinesthetic Intelligence "Body Smart": These individuals do very well in physical activities such as sports, dance, and acting. They might be found moving, twitching, tapping, or fidgeting while seated for a long period. They learn best by doing and often exhibit good fine-motor coordination (e.g., woodworking, sewing, mechanics).

Musical Intelligence "Music Smart": These learners are sensitive and talented in musical expression, rhythm, pitch, and melody. Students have a rhythmic way of speaking and/or moving as well as being sensitive to environmental noises (e.g., car horns or rain on the roof). They enjoy singing in a choir or joining other musical groups (e.g., playing percussion instruments).

Interpersonal Intelligence "People Smart": People who exhibit this intelligence have the ability to perceive and understand the moods, intentions, motivations, and feelings of other people. They enjoy socializing with peers and belonging to clubs, committees, and other organizations (younger children seem to be part of a regular social group).

These people are very empathetic and can accurately express how they feel. They are social learners and benefit most from cooperative learning strategies.

Intrapersonal Intelligence "Self Smart": These learners know themselves well and display a sense of independence and strong will. They work well independently or in small groups. You might need to spend some time with this child to find out about his or her hobbies and interests. These children are able to learn from their success and failures in life and exhibit high self-esteem.

Key Points in Multiple Intelligences Theory

1. Each person possesses all seven intelligences.

2. Most people can develop each intelligence to an adequate level of competency.

3. Intelligences usually work together in complex ways.

4. There may be more than seven kinds of intelligence.

5. Effective education should honor these differences among children, teach with the various intelligences in mind, and assess students' strengths and weaknesses in ways that are "intelligence fair."

6. The concept of multiple intelligences is diametrically opposed to the theory of general intelligence or IQ scores.

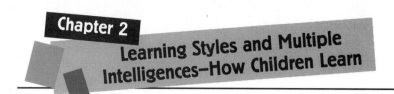
Using Learning Centers That Support Each of the Multiple Intelligences

An approach that is being used more often in the elementary grades is organizing learning centers that are dedicated to specific intelligences. Learning or activity centers can take on a variety of forms. Following are examples of how learning centers can be organized and the activities that can support each center's objectives:

Linguistic Center

- Area for books and magazines—comfortable chairs, beanbags, loft, etc., with tape player and earphones for taped books and posters that promote reading for enjoyment

- Writing area—large or small tables, typewriters, computer, and pencil and paper

- Board games—e.g., Scrabble® and Boggle®

Logical-Mathematical Center

- Math activities—calculators, worksheets, manipulatives

- Class store—where students can "buy" items, computing cost and sales tax

- Science area—simple experiments, books, and videos

- Games—e.g., dominoes, Uno®, Sorry®, Monopoly®

Spatial Center

- Art projects—drawing materials, collage materials, clay, "how to draw" books, and table loom

- Games—Pictionary®, Connect Four®, Lincoln Logs®, and Legos®

- Visual media—videotapes, maps, and puzzles

Bodily-Kinesthetic Center

- Open space—with rug for movement activities, e.g., mini-trampoline, Twister®

- Drama center—puppets, costumes, and Roll a Role* game

- Hands-on activities—blocks, sandpaper and wood, tools for dismantling an old appliance

Musical Center

- Music lab—cassettes, earphones, and tapes

- Performance area—electric keyboard, earphones, percussion instruments, rhythm machine, homemade instruments

Interpersonal Center

- Round table—for small group activities and discussion

- Socialization games—Roll a Role*, Ungame, Life Stories

- Communication skills—"Talking on Purpose," tape recorder

Intrapersonal Center

- Individual desks and/or study carrels

- Area for "alone work"—loft or corner with partition

* *You can order Roll a Role from Youth Specialties, 1224 Greenfield Dr., El Cajon, CA 92021. (619) 440-2333. And "Talking on Purpose" from Communication Associates, P. O. Box 586249, Oceanside, CA 92058. (619) 758-9593.*

Setting Up Learning Centers

Each learning center should be clearly labeled (e.g., "Word Smart Center" or "Art Smart Center"). One method of labeling is to laminate the signs and on the backs put Velcro® tabs . This makes it easier to "move centers" when needed. Centers are named for the intelligence that is used most in that area; integration of different intelligences will naturally occur (e.g., drawing a picture for a poem they wrote in the "Word Smart Center").

How to Introduce Students to Learning Centers

Students should be given information throughout the year on the different types of learning styles and intelligences they share. This can be achieved through discussion as well as activity sheets, such as "Looking at Learning Styles" and "Finding Out My Preferred Learning Style," located at the end of this chapter. One teacher made a game out of guessing "what intelligences are used in these areas?" and then asked the students to put the correct labels on the corresponding centers. Introducing one center or intelligence at a time, while letting each student try one of the activities available, is another option. Whatever method you choose to introduce centers, your enthusiasm about getting started should be felt and shared by the students.

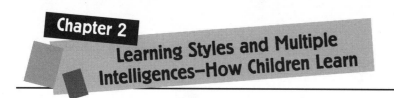
How Do Students Choose Where to Go and What to Do?

There are several ways you can approach the idea of learning centers that address the unique intelligences of each child. Each day can be dedicated to several areas of intelligences. Students can spend time at different centers selecting activities they choose. There can also be a day(s) of teacher-directed activities. Once you the teacher becomes familiar with the different learning styles and unique intelligences of your students, you can direct them to different areas.

It is also an option to combine centers and at times offer children open-ended activities. Games such as Scrabble®, Twister®, and Monopoly® lend themselves well to open-activity centers. Open-ended centers are also useful for introducing students to the idea of multiple intelligences.

In addition, learning centers can be made available to students after they've completed their other schoolwork or during break and recess times. When used in this way, information pertaining to their preferred intelligences can be easily collected. For example, students who always gravitate toward the "Word Smart" area and engage in reading and writing activities convey to you the importance of written language in their lives.

Integrated Learning Curriculum Centers

Another approach to integrated learning is to choose a topic or theme for all centers, which could last for a day, week, or month. For example, the topic could be "Cloud Formations." Each center would have written instructions on how to contribute to this class theme.

Word Smart Center

Please choose an assignment:

- Read and then write about how clouds are formed.
- Write a poem about clouds.
- Describe what it would be like to be inside a cloud.
- Make up your own activity.

Art Smart Center

Please choose an assignment:

- Make a display of cloud formations, using cotton, glue, and tag board.

- Draw a colored illustration of the water cycle.

- Design a new type of cloud formation.

- Make up your own activity.

People Smart Center

Please choose an assignment:

- Discuss with a learning partner how to identify cloud formations.

- Have a group discussion about how clouds are formed and select a spokesperson to summarize your conclusions to the entire class.

- Make a list of five different cloud formations and let each student choose one and share all he or she knows about it.

- Make up your own activity.

Music Smart Center

Please choose an assignment:

- Make up a rap song about how clouds are formed.

- Pick out different musical instruments that sound like the different cloud formations.

- Make up your own activity.

Learning Centers can stimulate a wide range of learning potential in students. The aforementioned descriptions have been structured to incorporate one intelligence per center, but there is no reason that centers cannot be structured to combine intelligences in a variety of ways. These suggested examples are just that, suggestions, and will hopefully stimulate your creative ability to design centers that support your students' success and involvement in the learning process.

Using a Seven-Day Lesson Plan to Integrate Support for Multiple Intelligences

Another approach to integrating support of the multiple intelligences theory in your daily curriculum is to develop a seven-day lesson plan that addresses a different intelligence each day. On pp. 31–32 is an example of what a seven-day lesson plan might look like for a regular forty-five-minute class weekly schedule. Poet Shel Silverstein was chosen for the example because of his contemporary feel, which is lively, fun, and child-centered. Children seem to easily engage themselves and become active participants in this style of poetry. Jack Prelutsky is another poet who writes fast-moving rhyming poetry that kids can easily relate to.

As you can see, the theory of multiple intelligences can be applied to the curriculum in many different ways. There are no standard guidelines. Reaching students through their individual learning styles and intelligences is the goal. If this approach to teaching a diverse population of children makes sense to you, then continue to explore and have fun creating additional ways to present information so that every child has the opportunity to succeed.

Sample Seven-Day
Multiple Intelligences Lesson Plan

Level:	6th Grade
Subject:	Language Arts
Objective:	Students will be introduced to Shel Silverstein's poetry and interpret its meaning.
Materials:	Overhead projector, transparencies, cassette player, art materials
Monday (Word Smart):	Read a poem to the students while their eyes are closed (this facilitates concentration on the poem itself). Then show the students the poem on the overhead projector and ask them to read it aloud together. Read the poem again while the students write down their own interpretations of the poem. Ask volunteers to share their interpretations with the class.
Tuesday (Number Smart):	Ask the students to divide the words of the poem into syllables. Explain that syllables determine the rhythm of the poem and beats per line. Have students clap hands to different beats or syllables. Present open-ended "Socratic" questioning to the students (e.g., "In what ways are _____ and _____ alike or different?" or "What would you do or say if you were _____?"). Answers can be discussed in pairs or written on paper first and then discussed.
Wednesday (Art Smart):	Write the poem on the chalkboard or on an overhead for the students to read. Hand out a variety of drawing materials (pencils, markers, crayons, etc.) and ask them to quick-draw the first image that comes to mind. Display the drawings and have each student interpret their drawing for the class, if they choose.
Thursday (Music Smart):	Bring in a variety of music (e.g., classical, jazz, rock, country). Ask students to bring in a favorite musical tape. Have volunteers read the Silverstein poem with different musical selections as background music. Ask students to listen and comment on how the mood of the poem changes when accompanied by the different music. Transcribe comments so they can be discussed after each reading.
Friday (Body Smart):	Form groups of four to six. Give each student a card with a section of the Silverstein poem written on it. As a group, perform the poem either through role-play, pantomime, or any other theatrical form.

Allow time for practice. A time limit should be set for each group's practices and performances.

Monday
(People Smart):

Divide students into groups of three to six. Ask them to write a group poem in a style similar to Shel Silverstein's. Give the theme of the poem—friendship. Then ask each group to have one person read the finished poem to the class.

Tuesday
(Self Smart):

Show students another Silverstein poem and ask them to find something (an image, word, sound, etc.) in the poem that means the most to them. Have them express their ideas in any mode of expression or form that seems right to them (e.g., writing, drawing, collage, song, dance).

Looking at Learning Styles

This activity can be used to introduce your students to the idea of different ways of learning. Begin this lesson with a discussion of learning styles by introducing these ideas:

1. "Because our brains are all a little different, we each have our own ways of learning. Each of us has things that come easily to us and other things that are more difficult to do or understand. For example, I have difficulty figuring out my taxes because of all the numbers involved, but I knit a sweater because I really enjoy working with my hands."

    • Discuss with your students things that are easier for them to do in school and at home and other activities that they find to be more difficult.

2. "The way we are most comfortable learning is called a learning style. Some of you learn easiest by seeing things with your eyes. You are visual learners. Those of you who learn best this way enjoy watching videotapes and filmstrips, looking at graphs, using webs, and seeing pictures of things you are learning."

    • Discuss any other activities that may be enjoyable to visual learners.

3. "Some of you learn easiest by listening. This is auditory learning because auditory means 'hearing.' Auditory learners really enjoy listening to stories, and they often can remember directions and people's names after hearing them only one time."

    • Discuss any other activities that auditory learners might enjoy, and why.

4. "Then there are those of you who learn best by moving and using your hands or bodies. This is kinesthetic, or tactile learning, because kinesthetic means 'movement' and tactile means 'feeling.' If you're a kinesthetic or tactile learner, you probably really like building, drawing, and doing things rather than listening or watching."

    • Discuss other possible activities these children might enjoy, and why.

Finding Out My Preferred
Learning Style

NAME_____ DATE_____

✔ Check the answer that is most like you.

1. ☐ I like to listen to stories and books on tape.
   ☐ I would rather read about things and look at pictures.

2. ☐ I remember the messages I hear.
   ☐ I like to write things down, otherwise I tend to forget them.

3. ☐ I like doing things with my hands.
   ☐ I prefer talking about things.

4. ☐ During my free time I like to be physically active and play a game.
   ☐ During free time I would rather draw, read, or write.

5. ☐ When I begin an activity, I like to take my time and think about what I'm about to do.
   ☐ I like to get things done quickly.

Now draw a picture or write about your favorite activity in the space below.

My Favorite Activity

CHAPTER 3
TEACHER TEAMWORK

When you are faced with the challenge of including children with a diversity of learning needs, disabilities, and unique gifts into your class of twenty (or maybe more!) children, it's inevitable that thoughts such as, "Can I reach all these children?" will enter your mind. The answer is yes, through conscious teamwork. The whole is truly greater than the sum of its parts. Collaborative teams are an essential part of the inclusion process. As teams meet, individual members begin to understand how their roles are interrelated to form a larger educational partnership.

In the teaching profession, the concept of teaming makes a lot of sense. An elementary teacher is expected to teach all core subjects, plan special activities, coordinate parent conferences, and now attempt to meet and cooperatively work with special education staff and specialists. At some point we begin to realize that we "cannot do it all." One of the main complaints from elementary teachers is that all "this" must get done with very little paraprofessional assistance, and with little or no prep time built into the week's schedule. These are very real concerns.

The classroom door can become a barrier, cutting off communication between the teacher and the rest of the school community. Teachers find that their classrooms can become a home away from home—a place where the entire day is filled up with the responsibilities of being a teacher.

Many teachers in schools across the country are realizing that *collaborative planning* is a way to decrease the isolation and barriers that are inherent in self-contained classrooms. There are many benefits as well as challenges when beginning the process of collaboration. The benefits do greatly outweigh the challenges, but the issues that accompany the teaming process are important to address.

Collaborative Teams

In some schools, the team consists of a regular and special education teacher, guidance counselor, school psychologist, parents or guardians, and student. Teams can begin with only two teachers, for example, the fourth- and fifth-grade teachers, and grow as desired. Try to keep the team size limited to five or six members. Many schools begin to include children who are nine or ten years old in team meetings. It's important to include the student, especially when he or she begins to show interest in knowing what is being discussed.

It will be very helpful if your school principal will support the teams and consequently arrange schedules to accommodate at least three forty-five-minute collaborative planning periods per week. This time can be filled with discussions concerning answers to problems team members face. Some elementary schools arrange for team time on Friday afternoons. A parent volunteer group can provide students with activities or an assembly every other Friday afternoon so teachers can meet with their team members. Some teachers need to arrange time before school starts to begin the collaborative process. Whatever the situation might be, scheduling is always a challenge for teachers who are committed to working together. As teachers begin to experience what it takes to make an inclusive classroom successful, the idea of working together to meet the challenges that arise becomes a priority. Many schools have developed creative approaches to developing cooperative teams and the time it involves to get started. Change happens, but it takes time and commitment.

Strategies for Working Well Together

Collaborative teams allow a group of concerned people to address issues and student needs that may be too large or too overwhelming for individuals to handle themselves.

Developing trust in each other encourages teachers to seek needed support. The team becomes a reflection of the cooperative values being taught in the classroom. In order to build trust among educators, all members must agree on a philosophy, which should include

- Meeting in teams will increase the development and opportunities for all students

- Meeting in teams will build a sense of collegiality among team members

- Meeting in teams will improve each member's ability to problem-solve creatively

In some middle schools, teachers are put into collaborative teams at the beginning of the school year, and team time is built into the weekly schedule. In other schools where this doesn't occur, teachers should look for other possible team members who have complementary teaching styles and personalities. An uncooperative person can create an imbalance that will affect the motivation of team members to work together. Consensus building is important for a team to be effective and for consensus building to occur there needs to be a balance among team members. Putting the effort into the initial stages of team building will only enhance the ability of members to reach their individual as well as group goals. Other factors that enhance the team effort include

- Lateral decision making
- Professionalism
- A shared desire to work together
- A professional respect for other's teaching styles
- A common vision that all students have the ability to succeed
- A sense of humor!

How Are Team Meetings Conducted?

Each team will take on its own personality as well as develop its own intrinsic and extrinsic rules of conduct. However, it's important to agree on some basic expectations that will guide the team process throughout the year.

These suggestions are the basis for developing an atmosphere of collaboration:

1. Meet in a large enough environment where all participants can see each other.

2. Introduce all team members by name and job title to parents.

3. When sending a written invitation to parents, arrange with a school secretary or guidance counselor to act as a facilitator for scheduling team meetings (get administrative support).

4. Encourage all members to arrive on time.

5. Welcome parents when they arrive.

6. Ask the parents if they have any specific issues that need to be addressed at the beginning of meeting.

7. Allow enough time for all members to share and offer comments without feeling rushed.

8. Get an idea of the goals and objectives for student(s) before the meeting starts. This can be done informally during the week at lunch times or recess, or by memos.

9. At the end of the meeting, check to make certain that all team participants understand the decisions agreed upon and identify any unfinished business that needs to be addressed at the next meeting.

10. Support the collaborative process by expressing your appreciation for the commitment team members have toward it. For example: "Mrs. Jordan, I appreciate your input and the concern you've shared about your son's grades. I'm certain with all of us working together as we've done so far, we will find ways to help him succeed."

You may find that one of the most enjoyable *and* challenging aspects of your teaching career will be co-teaching or working collaboratively with colleagues in the classroom. Co-teaching has helped many teachers realize a few very important personal truths that are worth sharing:

Co-teaching is:

- Planning lessons together

- An opportunity for two teachers to create an exciting learning environment

- Two teachers working cooperatively in the regular classroom

- Not a way to judge or criticize another teacher's style or skills

- Not the sole solution to inclusion in the regular classroom

- A commitment to working through any conflicts or problems that arise

- A learning process
- Worth the work

Collaborative teaming is analogous to the development of inclusive classrooms in that it is ongoing. As teachers begin to understand the process of brainstorming, which allows for multiple solutions, each meeting becomes its own adventure. Any needed changes to the process can be worked out over the course of time. Teacher ideas can be implemented, tried, and changed when necessary. The "Team Meeting Planning Form," p. 41, was developed to help ensure an efficient use of team time.

When you begin to co-teach, it's important to allow time for planning. What would it be like if a professional football team began a game without having agreed to any plays?

The quarterback would probably try to look as if he knows what he's doing so the other team doesn't catch on. Some passes would be completed out of chance and maybe a few points would be scored. The rest of the players would probably try to keep out of each other's way and anxiously look forward to the game being over.

This unlikely scenario is not that different than two teachers attempting to co-teach without planning. As teams begin to function smoothly by gaining experience, the need for daily structured team planning may lessen. Collaborative planning time is certainly a challenge to both regular and special educators as more students with special needs are being served in the regular classroom. However, if teachers are to collaborate for the benefit of all students, they must find the time to meet and share information. The "Co-Teaching Planning Forms," pp. 42–44, can facilitate productive planning time.

Roles, Responsibilities, and Options

Co-teacher roles and responsibilities are going to be different. Everyone has and prefers to use his or her individual strengths. One of the great benefits of a co-teaching model is that it allows the individual teacher to do what he or she *does best*. This also can be an opportunity for students to observe how eachers or adults

tcan appreciate their own differences and support each other's strengths. The message that everyone has something he or she does best and something special to contribute will be clear in a successful co-teaching experience.

For example, say an English teacher on your team has strengths that are different from yours. When teaching a unit in novel reading, for example, you set aside time each week for everyone to read out loud. After every few pages ask comprehension questions to check for understanding. During your co-planning time, read the novel and call on others to do the same while the English teacher asks comprehension questions. This helps acknowledge your individual teaching styles and strengths, and utilize them to the fullest.

The increased flexibility of elementary and middle-school curricula and structuring of classroom practices permits a creative co-teaching experience. It is also becoming increasingly more acceptable among classroom teachers to allow children to work at their own pace and on the different topics and learn in different ways. In many schools the special education teachers team teach in the classrooms—working as co-teachers with some teachers throughout the year, and in a consulting capacity with others. Instructional aides can provide direct service, support, and monitoring of the underachieving students. Although they are usually directly supervised by the special educator, they can assist *all* staff.

Pull-out services can be effective as well. You may utilize the resource room or "Student Learning Center" to address the stated Individual Education Plan (IEP) goals (reading, writing, and math) while working with students in small groups. In keeping with the inclusive classroom philosophy, include regular education students who need extra help. When co-planning with the math teacher, for example, schedule two "pull-out" periods per week. Elementary and middle-school students are often eager to work in a resource room that can offer small-group instruction. There are times when students with learning disabilities need to work in an environment where there are few distractions, especially when working on new or challenging material. They can be more focused in a resource room setting for part of their instruction.

Author's Experience

Recently, my school system has developed Student Learning Centers (SLCs) in all elementary and middle schools. The SLC is for students who need additional assistance with classroom assignments, projects, homework, and so on. It is this type of flexibility that creates an atmosphere of acceptance for all learners within the mainstream of the school community.

Team Meeting Planning Form

School _____ Grade _____ Date _____

Team Members in Attendance:

_____   _____

_____   _____

_____   _____

The parents _____ will or _____ will not attend.

The agenda for this meeting is (include names of student[s]):

_____

_____

_____

Teacher concerns:

_____

_____

_____

Parent concerns:

_____

_____

_____

Implementations:

_____

_____

_____

_____

_____

_____

_____

_____

_____

Co-Teaching Planning Form

Teachers:

Subject Area _____

Date _____

_____

_____

_____

Lessons Objective(s):

Materials Needed:

Activities: **Teacher Responsible:**

1. _____   _____

2. _____   _____

3. _____   _____

4. _____   _____

Student(s)   **Adaptations/Modifications**

1. _____   _____

2. _____   _____

3. _____   _____

4. _____   _____

Observations and Comments:

Co-Teaching Planning Form

Teachers:

_____Ms. Thoa_____

_____Mr. Khalsa_____

_____

Subject Area ___Math (Graphs)___

Date _____3/91_____

Lessons Objective(s):

— To increase understanding and use of a bar graph.

— Have students work cooperatively to show and compare cars teachers drive

Materials Needed:

— Paper, graph paper, writing and drawing materials, rulers, crayons, markers

Activities:	**Teacher Responsible:**
1. Introduce bar graph and lesson	Mr. Khalsa
2. Data Collection, stem and leaf	Ms. Thoa
3. Review graph set-up/collect data	Mr. Khalsa, Ms. Thoa
4. Design graphs using data, display	Mr. Khalsa, Ms. Thoa

Student(s)	**Adaptations/Modifications**
1. Joseph S.	— Assist with drawing lines on graph paper.
2. Luis A.	— Pair with a learning partner
3. Kathy S.	who comprehends objective.
4. Michael D.	

Observations and Comments:

— Students tend to comprehend bar graphs more readily than other forms of graphs and tend to enjoy making them when given a choice.

— Studnets are able to verbalize (or graph) about what they can actually see. "I see more teachers drive Toyotas than Fords, etc."

Co-Teaching Evaluation Form

Please answer the questions that apply to you and your co-teaching experience.

Name (optional) _____   Date _____

School _____   Grade _____

Teaching Position (special or regular education, instructional aide, other):_____

_____

When did your co-teaching team plan together? _____

_____

For how long?_____

Suggestions for co-planning:

_____

_____

_____

_____

Personal benefits of co-teaching:

_____

_____

_____

_____

Suggestions for improving co-teaching:

_____

_____

_____

_____

Next semester/year, I would prefer to:

_____ continue with my team and co-teacher(s)

_____ change my team and co-teacher(s)

_____ other:

From *The Inclusive Classroom.* Copyright © 1999 Good Year Books.

Student Introduction Form (confidential)

Student _____ Grade _____ D.O.B. _____

This form was completed by_____ Date _____

What are the approximate independent functioning grade levels?

Reading _____ Social Skills _____

Math _____ Classroom Behavior _____

Spelling _____ Other Subject(s) _____

Describe any physical limitations that may require any classroom adaptations/modifications:

Vision _____

Hearing _____

Motor _____

General Health _____

Other _____

Check the student's preferred learning style(s):

_____ Visual   _____ Tactile (hands-on activities)

_____ Auditory   _____ Kinesthetic (whole-body involvement)

(additional information) _____

Check the student's work habits in the classroom:

_____ Works independently

_____ Needs extra time on classwork

_____ Needs occasional prompting to stay on task

_____ Is usually late for class

_____ Easily distracted by loud sounds, talking, etc.

_____ Asks for help when needed

_____ Needs help with organizing classwork, notebook, homework, etc.

_____ Gives up easily

Works best when:

_____ Working with peers   _____ Needs to move about occasionally

_____ Working alone   _____ Tends to be an impulsive learner

_____ Working with an adult   _____ Tends to be a passive learner

_____ Working in a cooperative team   _____ Tends to be an active learner

Student Introduction Form (confidential)

Student _____Sarah_____ Grade ___5___ D.O.B. __11-15-85__

This form was completed by __Sp. Ed. Teacher__ Date __8-15-96__

What are the approximate independent functioning grade levels?

Reading _approx. 2 grade_ Social Skills _2-3 grade level_

Math _approx. 3 grade_ Classroom Behavior _2-3 grade level_

Spelling _2.5 grade_ Other Subject(s) __N/A__

Describe any physical limitations that may require any classroom adaptations/modifications:

Vision _____wears glasses_____

Hearing _____normal_____

Motor _____—_____

General Health _complains of stomach aches, otherwise normal_

Other _____uses inhaler for relief of allergies_____

Check the student's preferred learning style(s):

____ Visual __X__ Tactile (hands-on activities)

__X__ Auditory ____ Kinesthetic (whole-body involvement)

(additional information) _____

Check the student's work habits in the classroom:

____ Works independently

__X__ Needs extra time on classwork

____ Needs occasional prompting to stay on task

____ Is usually late for class

__X__ Easily distracted by loud sounds, talking, etc.

__X__ Asks for help when needed

__X__ Needs help with organizing classwork, notebook, homework, etc.

____ Gives up easily

Works best when:

__X__ Working with peers ____ Needs to move about occasionally

____ Working alone ____ Tends to be an impulsive learner

__X__ Working with an adult __X__ Tends to be a passive learner

__X__ Working in a cooperative team ____ Tends to be an active learner

Student Modification Worksheet

Student _____ Grade _____ Date _____

Regular Classroom Teacher _____

Special Education Teacher/Personnel _____

List the subject area and describe modifications needed.

Regular Education Activity/Content	Options* 0-4	Modifications Needed Description of Considerations	IEP Goals

*Modification Options

0–No Adaptation/Modification Needed

1–Reinforcing the Activity/Content

2–Adapting/Modifying the Activity or Content

3–Developing Parallel Activity or Content

4–Developing Alternative Activity or Outcome

Student Modification Worksheet

Student ___Chris M.___ Grade __1__ Date __3-14-96__

Regular Classroom Teacher ___Reg. Ed. Teacher___

Special Education Teacher/Personnel ___Sp. Ed. Teacher___

List the subject area and describe modifications needed.

Regular Education Activity/Content	Options* 0-4	Modifications Needed Description of Considerations	IEP Goals
Tests	2	Extra time-may need to complete in Resource Rm. Vocab. list for questions	2a
Essays/Reports	1/2	May need extra time to complete. visual aides, use of peer buddy for guide	2b,c
Classroom Behavior	2	Ignore non-compliant behavior. Give encouragement and praise frequently for cooperation.	1a
In Class Reading	0		
Homework Organization Skills	2	Simplify directions Check assignment book daily	3a,b

*Modification Options

0–No Adaptation/Modification Needed

1–Reinforcing the Activity/Content

2–Adapting/Modifying the Activity or Content

3–Developing Parallel Activity or Content

4–Developing Alternative Activity or Outcome

SAMPLE—Staff Questionnaire on Special Education and Inclusion at Kennedy Middle School

As many of you know, today's schools are undergoing a re-evaluation and restructuring of how to effectively educate all students, especially those who have an inability to learn in traditional ways. Regarding special education, the trend is toward developing a partnership of special and general education teachers. Some of the staff at Kennedy have already experienced the benefits as well as the challenges of this partnership. With the understanding that the success of inclusive programs is based on **cooperation, communication,** and **commitment** to the process, we are asking you to fill out this short questionnaire, which will give us information for a workshop we are developing on this topic.

Circle the number that best reflects your belief.
(Please return questionnaire to the teacher who gave it to you. Thank you.)

1–Strongly Agree   2–Mildly Agree   3–Mildly Disagree   4–Strongly Disagree

1. Inclusion is:

    - For students who would previously have been served by special education classrooms, but now may benefit in regular classrooms 1–2–3–4

    - Special education and general education staff working together as a team in the same classroom 1–2–3–4

    - Special education staff and general education teachers planning lessons together 1–2–3–4

    - All students learning at the same time, at the same pace, and in the same way 1–2–3–4

    - A favor from one teacher to another to work with students with special needs 1–2–3–4

    - For all students with Individual Education Plans 1–2–3–4

    - Sacrificing quality education of regular education students 1–2–3–4

    - Using classroom and curriculum modifications so that the opportunity for attainment of success is available to each student 1–2–3–4

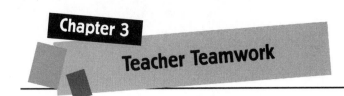

2. *Students with:*

- Learning disabilities should be included in the regular classroom 1–2–3–4

- Attention deficit/hyperactivity disorder should be in the regular classroom 1–2–3–4

- Mental handicaps should be included in the regular classroom 1–2–3–4

- Behavior problems should be included in the regular classroom 1–2–3–4

- Physical handicaps should be included in the regular classroom 1–2–3–4

3. *Select three topics you'd like covered in a workshop(s):*

(a) Understanding the Law: PL94–142 and IDEA
(Indiv. with Disabilities Ed. Act)

(b) Increasing awareness of the challenges faced by those with disabilities

(c) Defining my beliefs about inclusion by looking at two opposing views

(d) Identifying the broad benefits that inclusion can bring

(e) Knowing when inclusion is appropriate

CHAPTER 4
MODIFICATIONS AND ADAPTATION— WHAT TO TEACH

This section focuses on helping teachers develop an understanding of not only what to teach when including all children in their classroom, but how to vary what they teach. Many of the modification suggestions are critical for the success of students with disabilities, especially those with learning disabilities. These modifications can also be considered when writing an Individual Educational Plan (IEP) and/or "Student Modification Worksheet," discussed in Chapter 3. The key element in determining the learning environment for an individual student is that student's IEP. The IEP is a plan with goals and objectives, specifically designed for an individual student, that takes into consideration the student's academic, social/emotional, and behavioral strengths and weaknesses, and designs an individual intervention program for that student. Many of these interventions consist of academic and environmental modifications. The "Student Modification Worksheet" is a tool that provides an easy-to-follow guide of the goals and modifications stated in the IEP.

How to Choose the Appropriate Modifications

Modifications and adaptations are changes in curriculum and classroom activities that accommodate the student with disabilities. They are needed in classwork, homework, assessment, the classroom environment, and interactions. Success cannot be guaranteed; but, it should also not be denied due to an inability to learn in traditional ways. Effective modifications bring success within the grasp of children who are otherwise denied it. A successful modification or adaptation will help the student bypass as best as possible his or her areas of disability.

Knowing how to choose the appropriate modification(s) as well as deciding if and when it should be implemented in the classroom, will take some co-planning. The following questions may be helpful when considering which modifications to use:

- What is the student's learning style(s) (e.g., visual, auditory, impulsive)?
- What are the activity or subject content expectations?
- What are the options for modifications and adaptations?
- Will content be given in the same manner to all students?
- How and when will the content be tested?
- Will alternative forms of assessment be used?

How Do We Begin?

To begin the process of deciding what modifications and adaptations would accommodate the student's full participation in the class, certain information about the student needs to be shared among team members. This information includes independent functioning grade levels, preferred learning style(s), work habits, physical limitations, and any modifications used in the past.

To facilitate this process, the "Student Introduction Form" (at the end of Chapter 3) can be used. This form will help create a student profile based on descriptions of services provided; instructional preferences and suggestions; preferred learning styles; and specific skill competencies in the areas of reading, writing, math, and social behavior. The special education teacher should complete this form with the student before or during the first few weeks of entering the regular classroom, and then review the form with all team members. The purpose of this form is to cooperatively meet the student's academic and behavioral needs.

Teachers need tools that will assist them in knowing a student's modification needs at a glance, and that act as a reference point from which they can build. This should be an informal but effective process for defining the child's individual needs within the regular classroom at both the elementary and middle-school levels. The "Student Modification Worksheet," can be used for this purpose. It provides:

1. A clear means of identifying specific areas in which the included student needs support;
2. A means of communicating needed modifications/adaptations among team members;
3. A method of identifying and integrating IEP goals into the regular classroom; and
4. A system of accountability for all teachers.

From *The Inclusive Classroom.* Copyright © 1999 Good Year Books.

Ongoing Collaboration

When the student has been integrated into the regular classroom, it's essential that the special education teacher maintain an ongoing dialogue with general classroom teacher(s) regarding the included student's progress. The "Daily Student Report," p. 62, can be used to facilitate this dialogue. It can be used daily, weekly, or on an "as needed basis."

Teachers who use this form have commented on its usefulness as well as the clarity it can bring to the collaborative process. Many times all that is needed to support a successful collaborative team effort is a system of communication and accountability. It is equally important that teachers agree to support this method of communication, establishing a relationship of mutual support.

Modified Lesson Designs and Case Studies

Lesson designs are included for instructional strategies that correspond to each area of modification. Children's learning styles and "intelligences" have been taken into account when writing these lessons designs. These lessons can provide a basis for teachers to work from. With ongoing collaboration, creative modifications or adaptations can be developed to meet an individual student's learning needs.

Classwork Modifications: Case Study

Sara's Story

Sara was included in Ms. Bernard's fourth grade. Her educational plan (IEP) referred to Sara as having difficulties in short-term or working memory, as well as following directions. When it came time to take a test, she became very anxious and would begin talking to other students. In reviewing her Student Introduction Form, Ms. Bernard also learned that Sara was primarily a visual learner.

The following are suggested modifications that could be implemented in the regular classroom to assist students having similar instructional needs:

Following Directions:

- Give directions in writing and verbally.

- Allow extra time for completion of work normally done in the classroom.

- Speak slower and paraphrase using similar language.

- Assign a "learning buddy" to facilitate following directions and comprehension.

- Increase amount of checking for understanding and guided practice.

- Keep instructions and presentations lively using visuals, graphics, and demonstrations.

- Use worksheets, calculators, and other visual materials to support learning style.

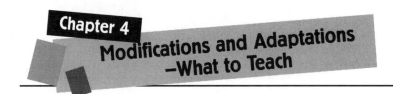

Memory Difficulties:

- Use acronyms (K.I.S.S. = "Keep it short and simple").

- Teach students how to make up fun sentences with the beginning letter of each word in the sentence standing for the information needing to be memorized in sequence. For example to remember notes on the musical staff (E, G, B, D, and F), students can remember the saying "Every Good Bird Does Fly."

- Ask the student(s) to repeat the information back to you or to a partner before beginning.

- Highlight concepts and information needed to learn.

- Expect use of assignment books.

- When reading, encourage use of sentence strips and word cards.

- Encourage use of graphic organizers (webs, outlines, etc.).

- Use a 10–2 structure, which means the teacher presents material for *ten minutes* then stops for *two minutes*. During the "pause," students pair up and help each other clarify concepts.

- Teach strategies that extend the time information will remain in the short-term memory such as:

1. **Rehearsal, or repeating the information.** When you repeat something, it slows down the process of forgetting and gives the information time to transfer into long-term memory. For example repeating a telephone number may help you to remember it long enough to dial it.

2. **Chunking or grouping information.** Grouping information is easier than remembering isolated bits of information. A good example of this strategy is how most of us have remembered our Social Security number, by chunking it into three groups: 123-45-6789.

3. **Making the information meaningful.** A child with memory difficulties needs to activate other parts of the brain to help retain the information coming in. For example, refer to a slice of pizza as a fraction, or part of the whole.

Assessment Modifications: Case Study

Joshua's Story

Joshua's education plan called for modified testing; specifically, this meant on essay-type exams. He had moderate to severe reading and writing difficulties. Whenever a test or quiz was mentioned, he would became anxious and would begin talking to a classmate or ask to go to the bathroom. When he entered Mr. Reese's fifth-grade classroom, the teacher noted that Joshua had difficulty paying attention.

Every child learns all the time. What they learn and what they do with what they learn needs to be assessed. Quality of work and individual student growth should provide a sound basis for student assessment. If it is accepted that all children learn at a different pace, at different times, and in different ways, it doesn't make sense to assess them all by the same standard. The following list of possible modifications and adaptations can be considered for students demonstrating learning difficulties.

- Prepare the student mentally and emotionally for the test by informally discussing it the day before, emphasizing its purpose versus grade importance. (See "A Helpful Hint for Teachers" at the end of this chapter.)

- Allow for oral testing to be given in the resource room.

- Make tests easy to read by eliminating unnecessary and confusing language.

- Provide multiple-choice or matching questions.

- Allow for extended time.

- Give test for homework as "study notes" in which questions are asked in a different way (e.g., Test: Who invented the telephone? Study notes: What did Alexander Graham Bell invent?).

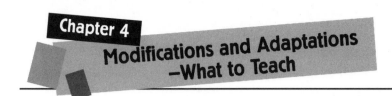
- Allow special education teacher to test student in a small group or individually.

- Read the test to the student; answers are written by the student.

- Have students keep a portfolio of their best work and encourage them to continue working on making those pieces better. At the end of the grading period, the portfolio is graded based on the quality of learning demonstrated.

- Enlarge print.

- Divide the test into short segments, and administer on different days.

- Have certain days for testing or "checking for understanding."

- Do not deduct for spelling, neatness, sentence structure, and so on, unless those are the things being tested.

- Allow student to retake tests and quizzes a second time.

- Give credit for what has been done correctly.

- Allow for student contracts. The contract outlines clearly what the teacher expects from the student. You may agree with students that "by completing X number of lessons, you'll receive an A, Y amount of work you'll receive a B," and so on. The terms of the contract should adjust as work progresses. Otherwise, students who initially overestimate their ability may become frustrated and discouraged from continuing. Likewise, students who underestimate their ability may lose incentive to work to their fullest capacity (see "Grading Contract" form, p. 73).

- Collaborate with special educators to rewrite tests for students with special needs. For example: shorter sentences, less questions, simplified vocabulary (see "Newton's Laws" worksheets, pp. 64-65).

- Avoid trick questions.

- Color-grade tests: **Blue** = "You understand it all," **Green** = "Nice work," **Brown** = "Needs improvement." Review color key with students before testing.

- Utilize pro-active grading. Students accumulate points based on what they accomplish rather than having errors count against them. This encourages students with learning difficulties to take more chances.

- Use tests to discover what the student has mastered and to determine what he or she needs to continue developing. Reduce weight of test grade.

- Give parents and students an option of receiving number grades or Pass/Fail. *Pass* indicates mastery of material; *Fail* indicates the need to continue working toward understanding. This system is especially effective in elementary grades.

- On math tests, allow the use of a multiplication table or calculator if assessing problem-solving skills.

> *"If it is accepted that all children learn at a different pace, at different times, and in different ways, it doesn't make sense to assess them all by the same standard."*

More Case Studies with Modified Lesson Designs

The following case studies and modified lesson designs are not only effective with students with special needs but with all children who have demonstrated a need for alternative teaching methods. Prior to referring a student for possible special education services, these modifications should first be initiated when appropriate. During the school year things will change: student enrollment, student competency/skill levels, and so on. Ensuring flexibility of student modification options is necessary. Even the most familiar modifications should be examined occasionally to determine their purpose, effectiveness, and appropriateness.

Case Studies: Adjusting to Individual Differences

Teaching and reaching all students in the inclusive classroom often requires altering the way one teaches. Useful modifications and adaptations already have been outlined in this chapter. These case studies offer a better understanding of how students with different disabilities in the same class can be reached.

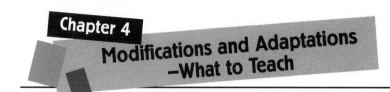
Ms. Holland's Fifth-Grade English Class

Ms. Holland has twenty-five students in her fifth-grade classroom. Of these twenty-five students, four are special education students. Sarah is legally blind; she has enough vision to enable her to move around the school environment with minor assistance. Jose and Rhonda are severely hearing impaired. Jonathan has been diagnosed with a mental disability and reads at about a second-grade level. All students are deficient in spelling skills. Mr. Mason, the special education teacher, consults and provides support to Ms. Holland.

Mr. Mason developed a program based on auditory sequencing for Sarah. He recorded the weekly spelling words one at a time on a cassette, emphasizing syllables and sequences of letters. For example: *dis-cuss, Wed-nes-day, at-ten-dance*. Each syllable pronounced independently can assist in spelling troublesome words. Sarah used the cassettes at a listening center with earphones while the rest of the class had spelling activities. She would listen to each word being spelled, dictate into the recorder the spelling of the word, and replay her spelling for comparison to the model words. She was also expected to use the cassettes at home.

To support Jose's and Rhonda's learning needs, Mr. Mason used a computer spelling program that presented spelling words on the monitor, emphasizing the visual sequences and configurations of letters. On a computer located in the classroom the students took turns typing in their own words that matched those on the program. Jonathan was given a shortened list of spelling words. The teaching and learning strategy Mr. Mason used required a multisensory approach. The strategy was first practiced with the entire class, then with a "study buddy," and, finally, completed as a homework assignment. The spelling instructions were written as follows:

1. Read one word at a time.

2. Spell the word out loud.

3. Close your eyes and spell the word while writing it in the air.

4. Write the word on your paper and check it.

5. Right? Write the word nine more times and then go to the next word.

6. Wrong? Go back to number **2**.

Memory techniques, or mnemonic devices, also were used with specific words. For example, with the word *Wed-nes-day*, each syllable is pronounced independently. Jonathan was told to remember that his attendance was expected at a dance that began at ten o'clock, thus becoming an *at ten dance*. In addition to these teaching techniques, his weekly spelling list was modified to reflect his reading grade level.

The class was also rehearsing for a holiday play that would be performed for the school. Jonathan really wanted to be in the play with his classmates. Ms. Holland was concerned that he would become frustrated reading his lines out loud due to his low reading level. Mr. Mason modified parts to reflect Jonathan's reading level, and they rehearsed the lines before reading them out loud in front of the class.

Mr. Powell's Fourth-Grade Math Class

Mr. Powell has five students with special needs in his fourth-grade class. Three students, Sammy, Lisa, and Noah, have learning disabilities. One student, Jessica, is visually impaired, and one other student, Angel, has been diagnosed with ADHD. All students find mathematics a difficult subject.

Jessica uses enlarged textbooks and writes with a marker on paper with darkened lines. She is seated close to the chalkboard and is allowed to walk to the board to see at any time. She also has a learning partner who is given carbon to put under her paper. When copying off the board, she makes a copy for Jessica. When talking to the class, Mr. Powell is careful not to stand in front of the window, especially on sunny days. The glare makes it difficult for Jessica to focus on him. When students do boardwork, Mr. Powell has each student orally review the steps to the problem. This provides review for the students and allows Jessica to hear each problem.

Sammy, Lisa, and Noah are given modified tests with fewer problems and simplified versions of the math concept being taught. For example, when testing long division or multiplication problems that involve several digits and regrouping, the teacher gives them problems with numbers for which most students know the math facts (e.g., 453 x 52 = ; most students know their times tables for 5 and 2). This way these students are tested on their *understanding* of the process and aren't penalized for poor memory skills.

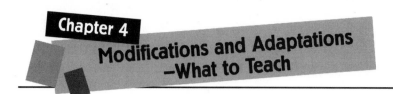
Mr. Powell has incorporated cooperative learning strategies that foster positive interdependence among all the students. Students in a cooperative group succeed only if every member of the group succeeds. Sammy, Lisa, and Noah are in three different groups. Team members check their material and answers. Information is shared, enabling them to review the concepts being taught. When Noah occasionally becomes extremely resistant to working with others, Mr. Powell offers a positive incentive or reward for cooperating.

Depending on the activity and his mood, Angel is allowed to work in a small group with other children or by himself. Mr. Powell makes a point of reviewing behavioral expectations with Angel prior to each activity. Angel uses a "Checking My Behavior" form (Chapter 6) that helps him monitor his classroom behavior. He is given short assignments (half-page, evens only, odds only) that are checked by a peer helper as well as by the teacher. When introducing or reinforcing new concepts, Mr. Powell provides multisensory instructions that include many kinds of manipulatives that can help Angel as well as the other students visualize and work out problems.

Meeting the instructional needs of children with diverse learning styles and disabilities often requires the classroom teacher to employ a variety of instructional methods. The manner in which you interact with your students, the environment you create, and the methods and curriculum you use to teach greatly affect how confident and successful your children will be in the classroom.

The following case study shows another teacher whose approach toward teaching in an inclusive class reflects some of the qualities and strategies needed to be effective.

Mrs. Flannders' Sixth-Grade Reading Class

Mrs. Flannders has four students with special needs in her sixth-grade reading class. Two students, Steve and Flora, have a reading disability. One student, Andrew, has been diagnosed with ADHD, and Cara, the fourth student, has a mental disability and reads at a first-grade level.

In the beginning of the class, Mrs. Flannders asked the students to get their materials for the instructional period. Andrew was given a word maze with the week's spelling words. This worksheet was on his desk before he was seated.

Mrs. Flannders moved to the sideboard that listed the period's activities, including a short vocabulary quiz. After identifying the period's objectives, she directed the students' attention to the board and briefly explained how the objectives were to be met. Her explanation reviewed what the class had done, how the day's work fit in, and what the next step would be.

Mrs. Flannders directed the group to get out their journals. The students were to write a short story, no longer than a few paragraphs, using the week's vocabulary words. She questioned different students and wrote their ideas for the story on the board. After checking for understanding of the assignment, she instructed the students to begin. As the group began writing, she gave Cara a sentence completion worksheet that included her modified vocabulary words. Cara, Steve, and Flora worked with learning partners who helped them with reading, spelling, and sentence structure. Andrew was working independently on finishing his word maze. Mrs. Flannders walked about the room. She helped individuals read their story and correct spelling and grammatical errors. She took aside four students who completed their assignment and had them correct one another's work.

As the rest of the students completed their project, the teacher had them pair off and correct one another's journal entries. Then she announced that it was time to prepare for the vocabulary quiz. Students moved into their specific groups, and worked with each other reviewing their vocabulary words for the week. Mrs. Flannders reviewed the modified words with Steve and Flora while checking on Andrew's and Cara's progress.

Mrs. Flannders praised individuals and the group for their appropriate behavior and cooperation. She passed out the vocabulary quiz, which consisted of matching the words to their correct definition. Steve and Flora had their learning partners read the definitions to them without disturbing others' concentration. Cara received the same test but was given the instructions to circle all the vowels in each word. Andrew's test was five words, and when he finished matching them to their definitions, he was instructed to draw a picture on the back of the paper illustrating the definition of one of the vocabulary words. He was also given colored markers to use as an additional incentive to complete the activity.

The students were instructed to pass in their papers at the end of the period. The transition between activities was smooth since the teacher gave cues to impending changes. She again praised individuals who completed their assignments and praised appropriate social and behavior work. As the period ended, the students were reminded of what they had done and what was coming up later that week.

Inclusive classroom teachers are open and willing to examine which factors need to be adjusted or modified in order for each student to achieve success. Chapter 5, *How to Succeed in Eight Lessons*, provides additional suggested modifications that will support the inclusive students' organization and self-esteem needs. Chapter 6, *Managing Behaviors in an Inclusive Classroom*, provides modifications used to support responsive classroom environments as well as successful student/teacher interactions.

Daily Student Report

Subject _____ **Date** _____

Regular   **Special**

Classroom Teacher _____ **Education Teacher** _____

Check whether the student's class/homework is complete or incomplete.

Student's Name	Complete	Incomplete	Comments/Modifications*

*Comments/Modifications:

– classroom behavior/attitude
– attendance
– test scores
– peer interactions
– additional information regarding modifications/adaptations

Daily Student Report

Subject _Math_   **Date** _3-14--96_

**Regular
Classroom Teacher** _Reg. Ed. Teacher_   **Special
Education Teacher** _Sp. Ed. Teacher_

Check whether the student's class/homework is complete or incomplete.

Student's Name	Complete	Incomplete	Comments/Modifications*
Javiar V.	✔		worked well with Jimmy C.
Mariza V.	✔		
Mark G.		✔	fifth day absent!
Jim C.	✔		
Ghalanda C.	✔		very cooperative today
Ananda K.	✔		worked well with Ghalanda
Ricky N.		✔	needs help with quiz
Don M.		✔	talking a lot with Lisa
Jessica G.	✔		15%, 90%, 85%-quizes last three
Mathew P.	✔		new seating arrangement has been helpful
Jose C.	✔		
Sue L.	✔		
Raja B.	✔	✔	does he wear glasses?
Lisa W.		✔	third day no h.w.
Montina E.	✔		study notes were helpful, 92% on quiz
Chris K.	✔		asked a lot of relevant questions

*Comments/Modifications:

- classroom behavior/attitude
- attendance
- test scores
- peer interactions
- additional information regarding modifications/adaptations

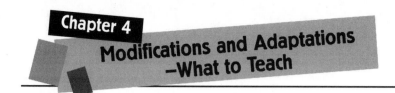

WORKSHEET

Newton's Laws of Motion
(BEFORE MODIFICATION)

The first Law of Motion states that if an object is at rest, it tends to remain at rest; if it is moving, it tends to keep on moving at the same speed and in the same direction.

The second law states that the acceleration of a body is directly proportional to the net force acting on the body, and inversely proportional to its mass:

$$A = \frac{F}{A} \text{ or } F = M \times A$$

The third law states when one object exerts a force on a second object (action), the second object exerts an equal and opposite force upon the first (reaction).

WORKSHEET

Newton's Laws of Motion
(AFTER MODIFICATION)

FIRST LAW: If an object is not moving, it will probably not move; if the object is moving, it will probably keep on moving at the same speed and in the same direction.

SECOND LAW: The more you push on something, the faster it goes, but the heavier it is, the slower it moves.

THIRD LAW: When one object pushes or pulls on a second object (ACTION), the second object pushes or pulls back equally (REACTION).

MODIFIED LESSON DESIGN

Language Arts

Subject:

Topic: Spelling/Vocabulary

Grades: 3–6

Objective: Improve spelling and sight vocabulary in daily writing and reading, using personal word banks

Activity: Students use a personal word bank to assist with their spelling and sight vocabulary while writing reports, reading stories, and so on.

Materials & Additional Resources:
- index cards
- small box for holding cards

Instructions:

1. Students are given index cards and a box to keep them in.

2. Every time the student reads an unfamiliar word, it's to be written down on an index card. The definition also can be written on the card.

3. The students can use, or "withdraw," these words from their bank when writing sentences, essays, and so on.

4. Spelling and vocabulary tests can be derived from words in the word bank.

MODIFIED LESSON DESIGN

Written Language

Subject:

Topic: Cursive Writing

Grades: 2–5

Objective: Introduce *cursive* writing to children who have mastered the formation of manuscript letters

Activity: Students practice cursive strokes through various exercises.

Materials & Additional Resources:
- felt-tip pen, colored pencil, or pencil
- paper with illustrations below

Instructions:

1. Children can be shown the similarity of manuscript to cursive writing by writing heavy cursive letters over the corresponding manuscript letters. This technique may be varied by using a different colored pencil or a felt-tip pen for the cursive letter.

2. Many of the cursive strokes can be practiced through games similar to those listed below. Have students practice by connecting the lines.

1.

2. *stringing the beads*

3. *making waves*

4. *lassoing the dots*

5. *making curly hair*

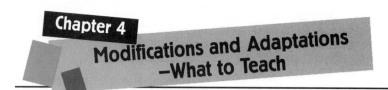
MODIFIED LESSON DESIGN

Mathematics

Subject:

Topic: Place Value

Grades: 3–6

Objective: Help teams of students understand place value

Activity: Students practice a variety of numerical place values in a game format.

Materials & Additional Resources:
- large index cards
- large felt-tip marker

Instructions:

1. Write numbers on large index cards with large felt-tip marker. Start with zero and number consecutively, depending on the degree of difficulty.

2. Divide class into two teams and give each student a card.

3. Each child holds a large number card as the teacher or an extra student calls out a number of two or more digits.

4. The children on each team with the called numbers move to a designated place corresponding to its place value.

5. The children stand in correct order to form the number. Every time a team forms a correct number, they win a check or point that is tallied on the chalkboard. This activity should have a set time limit.

MODIFIED LESSON DESIGN

Subject: # Mathematics

Topic: Basic Computation

Grades: 2–5

Objective: Practice basic computation skills and improve target accuracy

Activity: Students practice a variety of computations using a game format.

Materials & Additional Resources:
- three shoe boxes
- stapler
- flashcards
- rubber ball or beanbag

Instructions:

1. Staple the ends of the three shoe boxes together so they are attached in a straight line.

2. Label each box with a different process sign, (e.g., plus +, minus –, and multiplication ×).

3. Place a group of flashcards in each box according to the process sign and appropriate degree of difficulty.

4. Students take turns bouncing a small rubber ball on the floor directed at one of the boxes. If a beanbag is used, the child aims directly into one of the boxes.

5. If the ball or beanbag lands in a box, the student takes a card from that box and answers the problem. If the answer is incorrect, the child can either choose another student to answer the problem or put the card back into the box and bounce the ball again.

6. You can use this activity as an informal assessment tool as well.

Popular Cooperative Learning Activities

Cooperative learning is not so much learning to cooperate as it is cooperating to learn.

Try these activities to increase learning in your class.

✔ **LEARNING BUDDIES.** Groups of two to four children meet together frequently to review for tests, ask questions, process material together, or translate information for practical understanding.

✔ **THINK • PAIR • SHARE.** Pair off children so they can discuss answers to questions with a classmate and then share their answers with the class.

✔ **THINK • PAIR • SQUARE.** This is the same as Think-Pair-Share, except that student pairs share their answers with members of another pair.

✔ **JIGSAW.** Using reading, spelling, math facts, or parts of an article or story, the teacher cuts lists or information into equal parts, one for each group member. Each student learns their own piece of information and then teaches or shares with other group members.

✔ **TEAM CHECK.** Students on a team help each other understand answers to exercises, so that any member of the team can be called upon to answer any one of the questions.

✔ **BRING & BRAG.** This strategy can be used instead of having the whole class listening to everyone's report, current events, show and tell, and so on. Instead each student shares in small groups of three to five students. After a few minutes of sharing time, students' names are randomly drawn from an envelope, and they tell the class about someone else's information.

✔ **ROVING REPORTER.** When a team gets stuck, one member roams the room looking for ideas and reports back to the group in a reasonable amount of time.

Example of an Original Math Test (Before Modifications)

MATH 6–CHAPTER 3 TEST

Estimate to the nearest dollar.

1. $13.45	2. $69.09	3. $8.90
48.90	– 34.44	× 77
+ 60.89		

Add.

4. 45.667
   + .558

5. 4.9 + 39.09 + 39.220 = _____

Subtract.

6. 50.09
   – 3.98

7. 55.09–33.80 = _____

Multiply.

8. 6.00
   × 75

9. 45.34 × 89.00 = _____

10. 68.09 × 33.33 = _____

Divide.

11. 5 ÷ 55.90 = _____

12. 6.9 ÷ 89.00 = _____

13. 0.3 ÷ 7.90 = _____

Solve.

14. A restaurant bought 6.8 kg of carrots at $0.90 per kilogram. How much did the carrots cost?

1. _____
2. _____
3. _____
4. _____
5. _____
6. _____
7. _____
8. _____
9. _____
10. _____
11. _____
12. _____
13. _____
14. _____

Example of a Modified Math Test

COMMENTS: When modifying a test, provide directions, examples, and necessary cues as reminders, as well as an ample amount of work space. Reduce the number of problems. Multiple-choice answers also are an option. Avoid having students transfer answers from one place to another.

MATH 6–CHAPTER 3 TEST

Directions: Show all of your work in the space provided. Be sure to check your answers.

Estimate problems 1–3 to the nearest dollar.

Example: $12.11   (Think): $12.00
              +10.98   +11.00
                                          $23.00

REMEMBER TO READ EACH SIGN CAREFULLY. YOU NEED TO DO A DIFFERENT OPERATION EACH TIME .

1.   13.45   2.   24.18   3. $3.23
      +48.90   – 12.78   × 5

ADD Problems 4–5. Remember to **line up** the decimal points.

Example: 2.3 + 4.9 = 2.3   4.   6.0   5. 3.0 + 2.9 + 1.8 = _____
                        + 4.9   +4.8
                        7.2

SUBTRACT Problems 6–7. Remember to **line up** the decimal points.

6.   5.09   7.   5.09 – 3.80 = _____
      –0.98

Grading Contract

Name _____ Date _____

Class _____ Grade _____

Category	Option 1	Option 2	Option 3	Option 4
TESTS	50%	40%	30%	25%
HOMEWORK	30%	30%	40%	40%
CLASSWORK	10%	20%	20%	25%
PERSONAL GOAL	10%	10%	10%	10%
TOTAL:	100%	100%	100%	100%
✔ MY CHOICE:	☐	☐	☐	☐

MY PERSONAL GOAL FOR THIS CLASS IS: _____

_____

_____

_____

I, _____, understand the grading option I have chosen for this marking period. I will stay with the option I chose until the end of this marking period, unless my teachers and I decide differently.

_____   _____
        Student   Teacher

Modification Checklist

To insure equal opportunities in the inclusive classroom, the following modifications are required:

Name _____ Grade _____

Special Educator _____ Date _____

Modification/Adaptation	Math	Reading	Science	Social Studies
1. Preferential Seating				
2. Visual Presentation				
3. Written and Verbal Presentation				
4. Extra Time for Completing Tasks				
5. Spelling Errors Not Graded				
6. Reduced Quantity of Homework				
7. Tests Modified				
8. Oral Tests				
9. Study Sheets/Guides				
10. Homework Club				
11. Learning Buddy				
12. Taped Texts				
13. Hands-on Presentation				
14. Assignment Book				
15. Reduced Copying from Chalkboard				
16. Computer-Assisted Instruction				
17. Encouragement of Participation				
18. Behavior Plan				
19. Other				
20. Other				

A Helpful Hint for Teachers

Children Who Avoid Taking Tests—Causes and Interventions

Many children with academic disabilities do not like taking tests and will do everything they can to avoid taking them. Due to their past failure and inability to achieve, they develop "test-avoident strategies," which on the surface can be mistaken for noncompliance or misbehavior. For example: as the teacher passes out the tests, the student might look at it and declare he or she is "not going to take this stupid test!" and crumple up the paper. Other things children might do to avoid taking tests might not be as apparent. These strategies include: asking to go to the bathroom, getting a drink of water, sharpening one's pencil, or talking to a classmate.

Awareness of the cause of these actions is the first step toward building the student's self-confidence. Additional steps include:

1. Using test modifications to keep failure to a minimum (e.g., fewer problems)

2. Modifying assessment of tests

3. Adapting the learning environment (e.g., testing in another room)

4. Reading directions to the child as well as writing them clearly on the testing

5. Preparing the student mentally and emotionally for the test by:
   a) Discussing how to approach it the day before
   b) Talking about its purpose versus grade importance

CHAPTER 5
HOW TO SUCCEED IN EIGHT LESSONS

Succeeding in school involves many skills that students with both special and general needs must acquire. These skills include: organizing, following directions, dealing with stress, and being responsible for personal behavior. This section is designed to meet the needs of these students, whether taught individually, in a small group, or in a classroom situation. This curriculum is based on the understanding that children do not always know instinctively how to succeed in school. These awareness skills are learned and require direct instruction.

The curriculum in this chapter can be successfully used with upper elementary and middle-school aged children (grades 3–7). Each lesson takes approximately one 45-minute period. Corresponding reproducible activity sheets are provided.

After the curriculum is completed, "refresher classes" can be taught on an as needed basis. The teacher can follow the format suggested or change it according to students' needs. These activities also promote the important personal quality of *self-esteem*. Although many authorities find that some children with learning disabilities have low self-esteem and interact inadequately with their teachers and classmates, all children regardless of their abilities and age need to internalize positive feelings about who they are. Developing a positive self-esteem will enhance the student's capability of managing life's challenges. Children who feel good about themselves usually express their feelings through their behavior as well as in an openness to learning and growing.

> *"Real education consists of drawing the best out of yourself. What better book can there be than the book of humanity."*
>
> —Mohandas K. Gandhi

Learning is an *active* process. This curriculum can be taught with inclusive classes that have students with a very wide range of learning styles and disabilities. It is essential to encourage students' active involvement by using teaching strategies such as role-play, cooperative groups, and learning partners. Studies indicate that through lectures and reading, a child's average retention rate is only 10 percent. When the teacher incorporates demonstration as well as group discussion into the lesson, the retention rate increases to 50 percent. When children practice by *doing*, their rate of retention reaches 75 percent and higher. At the end of this section are many worksheets and activities for the eight lessons that follow.

Lesson 1: Positive Role Models (Use Activity Sheets 1 and 2, pp. 83–84.)

Before starting the first lesson, facilitate a class discussion of the purpose of this unit. The following are some ground rules for the class discussion:

- All students are encouraged to participate but have the freedom to respond or not respond, without the fear of judgment or pressure from others.

- Support and encouragement from teachers and classmates is expected.

- Respect and appreciation for diversity (ethnicity, culture, learning styles, etc.) are also expected.

This first lesson addresses the importance of children having positive role models. Children who lack role models tend to get confused easily. Having the correct books in class, or keeping track of their belongings, can often be challenging. These children tend to be quite disorganized and messy. When their desks become disaster areas or their lockers begin to resemble a trash bin, they are required to straighten them, but usually take an exceedingly long time to do so and still have difficulty organizing them in a logical manner. These children also have a difficult time making decisions. When asked simple questions, they will often shrug and respond with "What do you mean?" or "I don't know." These children should not be labeled "of low intelligence," or learning disabled.

Establishing positive roles models includes the following steps:

- **Helping children understand what they believe**. The values and beliefs that children have can act as guides for their personal behavior in school and at home.

- **Guiding children to set reasonable and achievable goals for themselves.** Children who have a lack of positive models are usually unsure of their goals. They need considerable help to clarify and work toward simple objectives such as hanging up their coats, taking out their books, determining how many math problems they will do for homework, and identifying what grades they want to get for the next marking period.

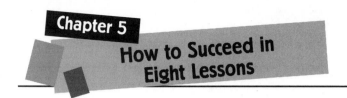
- **Expose students to successful role models.** Be careful not to fall into the trap of "Do as I say; not as I do." Children benefit from seeing responsible behaviors in addition to discussing and practicing them through role-play activities. To facilitate awareness of positive role models, you can use Activity Sheet #1, "Characteristics of People I Like," or invite into class other faculty members as guest speakers who will share the values and beliefs that guide them in life. You can also use videos such as Michael Jordan's *Come Fly with Me*, to illustrate positive role models for many children. In the beginning of this video he shares how the values of working hard for what you want and having the determination to succeed and never give up, have guided him toward his personal success as an athlete and businessman. If time allows, show the video in its entirety at the end of the lesson or the next day. Children never seem to get tired of watching him play basketball! Then do Activity Sheet #2, "Come Fly with Me."

Lesson 2: A Safe, Comfortable Learning Environment
(Use Activity Sheets 3 and 4, pp. 85–86.)

Discuss the importance of being relaxed and comfortable at school. Children often need encouragement to discuss times they have felt stressed, relaxed, or comfortable at school. In order for students to take risks in class and fully participate in the learning process, they must feel safe and relaxed in their school environment. Students must be able to identify when they're feeling stressed and learn ways to manage their stress during and after school. Both students and teachers can practice simple techniques to release their stress within a classroom setting. This is especially important for kinesthetic learners.

Help children fill out the "Ways to Manage My Stress" activity sheet, which encourages them to look at how they deal with daily stress. Also try the "Stress Away" activity, which encourages children to practice a relaxation method by using the stress control cards. This is a very enjoyable activity that also can be a great way to begin each school day.

Lesson 3: Making Friends (Use Activity Sheets, 5, 6, 7, pp. 87–89.)

Developing and maintaining friendships is the foundation of an accepting, inclusive classroom. A major factor in being comfortable in school is feeling connected to others, or having friends. Teachers can help create a caring classroom that embraces the philosophy that all children are special and unique. These three activities (5, 6, 7) promote the understanding that one should not judge someone by their outer appearance. Children are encouraged to get to know each other in a fun and nonthreatening way. After the written responses are completed, it is important to generate a discussion about what children wrote.

Lesson 4: Organization Skills (Use Activity Sheet 8, p. 90.)

Many children with learning disabilities could learn better if they were better organized. Learning would be easier as well as more enjoyable, if students kept track of their materials and remembered the things they were supposed to do. Getting organized takes conscious planning as well as changing some poor habits. This lesson will first help increase students' awareness of their present organizing habits. These activities will then offer some effective strategies that can improve organization.

Begin this lesson by asking students what it means to organize themselves. Discuss their answers and make a list of their responses on the board. Point out the different and similar answers. Help generate a discussion regarding the importance of self-organization and the possible consequences of being and not being organized (e.g., being organized means getting work done on time, getting better grades, feeling better about self. Not being organized means more difficulty in learning, feeling frustrated, getting poor grades, etc.). Next, hand out the Activity Sheet 8, "Organizing Myself," and follow with more discussion.

Lesson 5: Listening to Others (Use Activity Sheets 9, 10, pp. 91–92.)

During this lesson, students discuss how listening to others may influence them to behave responsibly. Teachers can define a *good listener* as someone who

- pays attention;
- knows what is said by repeating it back; and
- does not interrupt or distract others when they are speaking.

After a short discussion of these definitions, students will then be ready for Activity Sheets 9 and 10, "Talk and Listen" and "Listening on Purpose." Each activity will take forty-five minutes to complete. Additional role-play experiences can enhance students' listening skills as well.

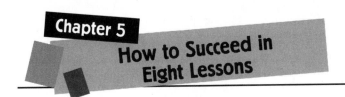
Lesson 6: Following Oral Directions
(Use Activity Sheets 11, 12, pp. 93–94.)

Begin this lesson by reviewing the differences between *listening* and *hearing*. To demonstrate the differences use these fun activities.

1. **"What is an aluminum can made out of?"** Ask for a volunteer to help demonstrate the difference between *hearing* and *listening*. Let them know that you're going to try to trick them by the questions you ask. "What is five plus five?" *Ten.* Nine plus one?" *Ten.* "Six plus four?" *Ten.* "What is an aluminum can made out of?" Most children will say, *Tin.* At this point we discuss why *tin* instead of *aluminum* was the response and that listening takes *full concentration.*

2. **"Simon says put your hand on your head . . ."** You can use your first or last name or "Simon." Children enjoy the challenge of this activity, and it gives students practice in listening and following oral directions. When doing this exercise, remember to point to a different part of your body after getting them used to touching the correct part of their body (e.g., saying "Simon says to touch your nose" while you touch your chin). Gradually increase the pace of directions so all children can feel challenged as they get the knack of it. Students who have coordination difficulties can be helpers by catching those who make a mistake.

The included student's difficulties with organization and following oral directions are probably the behaviors teachers cite as most troublesome. The reason children have difficulty following directions is often poor listening skills, also defined as poor critical listening. It is not unusual for a teacher to give clear and simple directions and have one or more students raise their hands and ask, "What do we do?" Activity Sheets 11 and 12, "Following Oral Directions" and "Listen Carefully—Then Draw," address this problem. These lessons focus on teaching strategies that will improve listening and following oral directions.

Lesson 7: Managing Classroom Attitude
(Use Activity Sheets 13, 14, 15, 16, 17, pp. 95–99.)

It is important that children understand "classroom etiquette." Understanding the consequences of classroom attitude will help children take responsibility for their behaviors. Begin this lesson with a discussion of the importance of students cooperating with their teachers. After this discussion students are asked to fill out Activity Sheet 13, "My Teacher and I." This part of the lesson is concluded with students discussing in small then large groups ways that they have previously cooperated with their teachers.

Activity Sheet 14, "Ten Ways to Manage My Classroom Attitude," gives students direct instructions on how to demonstrate a positive learning attitude in the classroom. After reading each statement to the class, students form small learning groups and read as well as role-play assigned statements. Activity Sheet 15, "A Better Way to Act," encourages students to use the information they've learned to determine the responsible way to act in class. Through discussion and/or role-play, students should share answers when finished. The "How Important Is My Attitude?" Activity Sheet 16, is a fun and intriguing mathematical exercise that can act as a catalyst for thought and discussion around the importance of one's attitude in school, at home, and in the community.

Understanding consequences of one's behavior is an essential part of succeeding in school. The "Flow Chart," Activity Sheet 17, can give the visual learner an opportunity to gain an added awareness of how a responsible behavior, such as doing homework, or an irresponsible behavior, such as not listening in class, can affect their ability to succeed in school.

Lesson 8: Review Progress (Use Activity Sheet 18, p. 100.)

Begin this final lesson by asking students to review some of the highlights of the previous seven lessons. Children describe what they have learned about themselves (e.g., "I learned that by organizing my things, I feel better about coming to school."). This process is facilitated by completing "Looking at My Progress," Activity Sheet 18. Teachers conclude the lesson by giving the students the opportunity to receive positive feedback from one another. The teacher can begin by modeling a descriptive compliment to a student. For example, instead of saying "Ananda, you did a good job," say "Ananda, you listened really well when I gave instructions."

This curriculum can have a significant and positive effect on children's awareness of how to succeed in school. In saying this, it should also be noted that not all special and general education students will show immediate improvement in the skills covered in

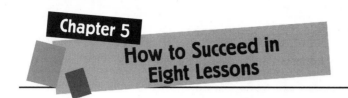

these lessons. Awareness of how to reach a goal does not automatically result in the achievement of that goal. However, many students not only enjoy participating in these lessons, but also gain a greater understanding of themselves as well as their school community. When students realize that these lessons can help them be more successful in school, they'll work harder to achieve that goal.

The importance of participating in this curriculum can be presented to students in this way: "If you're having difficulties learning in class, you may not enjoy coming to school. You may not like school at all. Can anyone tell me what the word *resist* means? To avoid failure, you might become what is called a *resistant learner.* You can go through school avoiding full participation, consequently feeling angry, frustrated, or sad. Participating in these lessons can change the way you feel about your ability to succeed in school. It can also give you a better understanding of what your unsuccessful school habits are, as well as how to replace them with successful ones. If you feel pretty good about school and are not having trouble learning, then this information will help you understand how to continue being successful in class. Any questions?"

Characteristics of People I Like

Name _____ Date _____

Directions

Define: *Characteristics*

Think about the people you like and look up to. Make a list of the characteristics of these people you admire. Next check "Yes" if you have the same characteristic or check "Like to" if you would like to have that characteristic. Then share your answers with your class. When you finish, put a check in the box at the bottom of the page.

Characteristics of People I Like	Yes	Like to
Example: My father has a good sense of humor.	✔	

☐ I completed this activity sheet.

Come Fly with Me

Name _____ Date _____

Directions

Define: *Attribute*

After watching the video of Michael Jordan, *Come Fly with Me*, answer the following questions. When you finish, put a check in the box at the bottom of the page.

1) Name three attributes of Michael Jordan that helped him to be successful.

    1. _____

    2. _____

    3. _____

2) Name three successes that you have experienced at school.

    1. _____

    2. _____

    3. _____

3) What successes do you expect to experience in the future?

    1. _____

    2. _____

    3. _____

☐ I answered all of the questions.

A Safe, Comfortable Learning Environment: Activity Sheet #3
Ways to Manage My Stress*

Name _____ Date _____

Directions

Please rate yourself on each question with a **5** for "most of the time"; a **3** for "sometimes"; or a **1** for "hardly ever." If your score is **37** or greater, you are doing great as far as finding ways of releasing stress in your life. If your score is below **25**, it's important to look at changing some of your habits (especially the "hardly evers").

I am succeeding at:

_____ 1. Scheduling time for fun activities.

_____ 2. Getting enough sleep at night.

_____ 3. Exercising every day.

_____ 4. Practicing relaxation.

_____ 5. Eating balanced meals.

_____ 6. Staying away from junk foods (candy, potato chips, soda).

_____ 7. Having a good laugh at least once a day.

_____ 8. Talking to someone about things that bother me.

_____ 9. Not letting things bother me so much.

_____ 10. Keeping up with my schoolwork.

Now score yourself by adding up your numbers.

* Used by permission of Professional Resource Press.

Stress Away[1]

Directions

If possible, obtain a Stress Release Card[2] for this activity. Otherwise the following sequence of muscle relaxation instructions can be used as an alternative to the directions on the stress control card. Begin by telling children that it's important to keep their muscles tensed for five to ten seconds and then release their tension and allow their muscles to go completely limp (you can use an analogy such as "wet spaghetti"). Wait twenty to thirty seconds before shifting to the next muscle group. Say the following directions in a slow, soft, soothing, repetitive voice. Any additional environmental changes, such as soft background music or dimming the lights, can also be helpful.

1. Have all students sit comfortably in a chair or lie in a comfortable position on the floor.

2. As you read these instructions, wait twenty to thirty seconds before moving on to the next muscle group.

   • Wrinkle your forehead and brow. Now slowly relax them.

   • Tense your eyes and face, squeezing the eyes very tightly. *Slowly* release, and enjoy the relaxed feeling. Let your eyes stay closed.

   • Now tense your jaw and press your tongue to the roof of your mouth. Slowly relax.

   • Bring your chin to your chest. Hold, then relax.

   • Pull your shoulders up to your ears. Hold, then slowly let go.

   • Make a fist with both hands. Squeeze, then release and let your hands open up.

   • Take a deep breath, pushing your chest out. Hold, now s–l–o–w–l–y let your breath out and relax your chest.

   • Tighten your upper legs or thighs. Let go of the tension.

   • Point your toes away from your head. Tense, then release and enjoy the relaxed feeling and go completely limp.

3. Now take a deep breath and hold it for a silent count of ten. When you let your breath out or exhale, let it all out at once, letting your body go limp.

If you are using a Stress Release Card, conclude by checking to see what color your card turned while I mark it next to your name on the chart.

---

[1] Used by permission of Professional Resource Press.

[2] Stress Release Cards can be ordered from BMI, Inc., 2387 East 8 Mile Road, Warren, MI 48091-2403. (800) 521-4640.

Making Friends: Activity Sheet #5

Can't Judge a Box by Its Cover*

(Depicted on this book's cover)

Materials: shoe box, wrapping paper, paper bag, dollar bill, undesirable object (e.g., old lemon, dried onion)

Directions

1. Prepare the shoe box by wrapping it as a present. Wrap it so the lid can come off and place the undesirable object inside. In the crumpled paper bag, place the dollar bill (or for younger children, use any age appropriate gift).

2. Then place the box and the bag in the center of the group circle and ask students, "If you could have whatever is in either container, who would choose the box? Who would choose the paper bag?"

3. Two children are chosen to first open up the box and show everyone its contents, and then do the same with the paper bag.

4. Now, all the students are encouraged to discuss the significance of what just occurred. Questions asked can include:

   • *What is the meaning of the saying "You can't judge a book by its cover"?*

   • *Who can explain what this activity has to do with getting to really know someone and making friends?*

   • *What are some ways you can get to know someone?*

5. During the discussion, take an active role in helping students explore alternative ways of getting to know someone. Using the metaphor of the box, emphasize the importance of getting to know someone by looking beyond their physical appearance.

6. When the discussion is completed, have students form pairs and fill out the activity sheet, "Getting to Know Someone." After partners share information with each other, volunteers are asked to share with the class what they learned about their partners.

---

* Used by permission of Professional Resource Press.

Getting to Know Someone

Name _____ Date _____

Directions

It often takes time to get to know more about someone than you might guess by the way he or she looks, talks, or acts. In this activity, pair off and then write on each line a personal statement about your partner. These things can include personal likes and dislikes, hobbies, etc.

Guess Who . . .

Directions

Answer the questions below without showing anyone what you've written. When everyone is finished, your teacher will read the answers and everyone will try to guess who wrote them. After everyone takes a turn guessing, your teacher will say something such as, "Will the person whose favorite food is . . . and finds it easy to do . . . please stand up." The student whose answers were just read will then stand up!

1. My favorite food is _____

2. My favorite TV show is _____

3. It is easy for me to _____

4. It is hard for me to _____

5. One of my friend's name is _____

6. I really enjoy _____

Organizing Myself

Directions

Getting organized for school is not always an easy task. If you need to get organized, try some of the ideas below.

1. Getting Ready for School

What is your daily routine? Maybe you get out of bed and take a shower before you get dressed. Or maybe you shower before going to bed and get dressed after you get up in the morning. Your regular way of doing things every day is called your "routine." A routine can make it easier for you to get organized. Here are some tips on creating a routine that can help you get ready for school:

✔ Get your clothes ready for school the night before.

✔ Check to see if you have all the books and materials you need to bring to school before going to bed.

✔ Ask someone to help you write down a weekly schedule of important things that need to get done. For example: "Tuesday, I need to bring in a jar for my science project." You can ask a parent, older brother, sister, or teacher to help you with this.

2. Using an Assignment Book

Assignment books are a great way to keep yourself organized! They help you remember what homework to do and which books to bring home. Here are some tips about how to use your assignment book.

✔ There are several types of assignment books. Some have one day printed on each page, and others have a few days printed on each page. Ask someone to help you decide which one works best for you. An assignment book that has a place where your parent can sign after you've completed the work is especially good.

✔ Open your assignment book as soon as you get to class. As soon as your teacher says what you'll need to do for the next day, write it down.

✔ Before going home, check your assignment book to see which books you'll need to take home.

Talk and Listen

Materials: small bell or cooking timer

Directions

1. Before beginning this activity, facilitate a class discussion about communication. Some points that should be covered include:

   - In communication there is always a speaker and a listener. What is the difference between speaking and listening?

   - When speaking, you should think about what you want to say and try to speak loudly enough (but without shouting), so the person can hear you.

   - When listening, try not to interrupt the person talking.

   - Try not to think about something else while listening.

2. After this discussion ask the students to sit in pairs, facing their partners. Each partner will take turns being a "listener" and then a "speaker."

3. Explain that the listeners will report what the speakers were saying, so it's important to really listen.

4. Each student will be given three minutes each to either *listen* or *talk* about the topic being discussed.

5. Ring the bell after three minutes, letting each pair finish their sentences or thoughts before changing roles to either a "listener" or "speaker."

6. After partners have taken turns, have students form a large group and share what each other said one at a time.

List of possible topics:

☆ "What I did on my last birthday"

☆ "A problem I need to solve"

☆ "My favorite subjects in school and why"

☆ "Three things that really bother me"

☆ "What I would do with $100"

☆ "My favorite dream . . ."

Listening on Purpose

Materials: audiocassette recorder (or a micro-recorder), chalkboard or newsprint

Directions

1. Ask students to sit in pairs and have a discussion about a favorite TV program.

2. While students are talking, inconspicuously move around the classroom and tape their conversations.

3. Then write "LISTEN" on the chalkboard and ask the class to stop talking and listen for a few moments to the tape recorder. Ask, "What is special about the way a tape recorder listens?" This helps the students understand that a recorder is very accurate and listens to every word just as it's said.

4. Have students sit in pairs and decide who will play the part of the tape recorder first. Have the "tape recorders" raise their hands. Announce that this is the topic to be discussed: "How would you spend $10?" The speakers begin talking and the "tape recorders" begin listening without speaking.

5. After one minute of talking, instruct the students to stop and switch roles, while repeating the same process, using the same topic. Then both students will have one minute to say what they heard, while the speakers listen.

Follow-up Discussion:

After the first minute of talking, ask the students these questions:

☆ What was it like to listen like a tape recorder?

☆ Speakers, how well did your "tape recorder" (listener) work?

☆ What was it like to be listened to so well?

☆ Why is it important to listen carefully when someone is talking?

☆ Why is it important to listen to your teacher? your parents? your friends?

Following Directions

Name _____ Date _____

Directions

Learning to follow directions will help you to do your work correctly and on time. Read the ideas below on following directions. Check the box next to each idea after you **remember** and **understand** what you've read. (You can have a choice of working alone or with a learning partner.) Your teacher will then check and see how many ideas for following directions you have remembered.

☐ After listening to the directions the teacher gives you, repeat the directions to yourself a few times.

☐ Write down the directions; it will help you remember them.

☐ Picture the directions you hear in your mind. For example, suppose your teacher tells everyone to find and circle the nouns in each sentence. Stop for a moment and in your mind picture yourself finding the nouns in a sentence and drawing an **O** around them.

☐ When your teacher is talking, listen for words that he or she repeats or says LOUDER. These words may be important direction words.

☐ Listen for these important direction words:

- **Listen**—"**Listen** to the sound this instrument makes."

- **Look**—"Before we begin, **look** at the picture on page six."

- **Write**—"I want you to **write** all the words on your paper."

- **Remember**—"**Remember** to study for the quiz tomorrow."

- **Circle**—"**Circle** all the nouns in each sentence."

- **Draw**—"After listening to the story, **draw** a picture of the house."

- **Do**—"**Do** all the problems on page twelve."

Listen Carefully—Then Draw

Materials: white unlined paper, pencil, ruler, cassette player optional

Directions

This is a fun activity that can help children (grades 3–7) follow directions. Students get an opportunity to follow oral directions and visually determine how well they did. Give the directions at a normal conversational rate of speaking. Use normal inflection and repeat each instruction once. You can also record each instruction and play it back as they draw. Give students enough time to complete each instruction.

I am going to give you directions for drawing a simple picture. I will repeat the directions one time, so it's important to listen very carefully to my directions. Now get ready.

1. In the middle of your paper, draw a square. It should be about 4 inches long and 4 inches high.

2. In the middle of your square, draw a smaller square. It should be about 3 inches long and 3 inches high.

3. Next draw a rectangle that is 6 inches long and 2 inches wide and touches the bottom of the larger square. The rectangle should be centered under the square.

4. Now in the upper right corner of the rectangle, draw a smaller rectangle about 1 inch long and 1/2 inch wide.

5. What did you draw? (answer: computer) Compare your picture with what the person next to you drew.

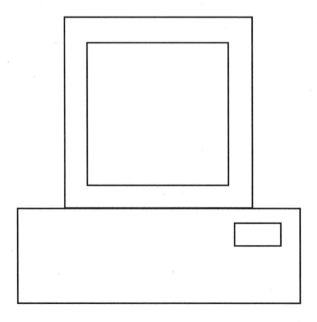

My Teacher and I

Name _____ Date _____

Directions

Getting along with your teachers is very important. It's also important that you show your teacher you are interested in learning. Read these **5 Great Tips** on ways to show your teacher you're interested in learning as well as being positive in class. After reading each statement, write it down. It will help you remember what you've read. Then pair up with a classmate and take turns telling each other a great tip!

1. When your teacher offers you help, remember to say "thank you." Your teacher appreciates it when you're polite. _____
   _____

2. If your teacher asks you a question and you're not sure of the answer, don't make negative comments, such as "I don't know" or "I can't." _____
   _____
   _____

3. Instead of making negative comments, make a positive comment, such as "I have to think about it" or "I don't know, but I'll try." _____
   _____
   _____

4. If you don't understand a question, raise your hand and say, "Can you please repeat what you said? I don't understand it." _____
   _____
   _____

5. Remember to say "good bye" to your teacher when you leave for the day.
   _____
   _____

10 Ways to Manage My Classroom Attitude

Name _____ Date _____

Directions

After reading each statement, work with one or two other partners and act out for the class a statement you've read. Take turns playing the role of teacher and student.

1. Pay attention to your teacher's voice. Notice when your teacher is trying to get your attention by talking louder, softer, pausing for a long time, or calling your name.

2. If your teacher asks everyone to pay attention and stop talking, be the first one to stop and wait until everyone is quiet before you ask a question.

3. Show your teacher you're interested in learning by sitting up straight in your chair, looking at the teacher, and ignoring others who are not paying attention.

4. Sit toward the front of the class. Don't sit next to someone who bothers you.

5. If you didn't do your homework, be honest and accept the consequences.

6. If you don't understand what your teacher is saying or need something repeated, ask your teacher politely. Tell your teacher you are having trouble keeping up.

7. Do extra credit work if the teacher allows it.

8. If you think you're getting blamed for something you didn't do, wait until after class to discuss it with your teacher. Don't argue with your teacher during class!

9. If you feel embarrassed about something that happened in class, talk to your teacher or your parents about it after school or during free time.

10. Practice being assertive, which means "to state one's opinion confidently and positively." Say what you mean without being loud or angry. For example: "I don't want to get in trouble so please stop talking to me."

From *The Inclusive Classroom*. Copyright © 1999 Good Year Books.

A Better Way to Act

Name _____ Date _____

Directions

Taking responsibility for how we act in school is not always the easiest thing to do, **but it is** always the right way to act. After reading the situations below, write what you think would be the best way to act.

1. Your teacher is covering a lot of material and seems to be going too fast. How do you ask your teacher to slow down? _____

    _____

2. Your teacher pauses for a long time. What does this mean? What should you do?

    _____

    _____

3. You don't understand something your teacher is explaining to the class. How do you let your teacher know? _____

    _____

4. Someone says something to you during class and you feel embarrassed. Who should you talk to about it and when? _____

    _____

5. You lost your homework and told your teacher. Your teacher still punishes you by having you do extra work at recess. What is the best way for you to react? _____

    _____

    _____

6. Someone sitting next to you keeps talking to you when they shouldn't. What is the best way to tell them to stop? _____

    _____

How Important Is My Attitude?

Name _____ Date _____

Directions

Your attitude, or the way you feel about something, is very important when it comes to being successful in school. But how important is it? In this activity assign a number to each letter in the word attitude. The number corresponds to the letter's place in the alphabet. For example, the letter "**A**" is the first letter of the alphabet so it gets a **#1** assigned to it, and so on. Then add up all the numbers and see **how important your attitude is.**

A _____

T _____

T _____

I _____

T _____

U _____

D _____

E _____ =

_____ %

The Flow Chart

Name _____ Date _____

☐ Responsible

☐ Not Responsible _____

Behavior

Directions

On the line above write the behavior you are going to chart. Check either *Responsible* or *Not Responsible*. Next, in each box below, write down the logical consequences to the behavior. For example:

Example:

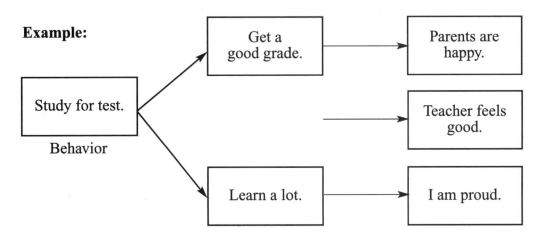

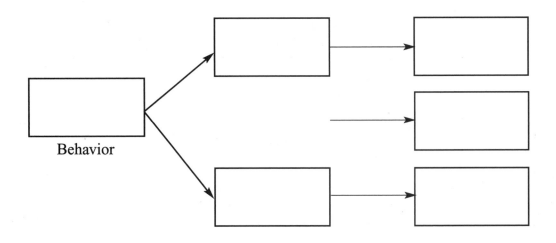

Looking at My Progress

Name _____ Date _____

Directions

Congratulations! You have learned the important tips to help you succeed in school. Now let's look back and see what you've learned. What are your strengths as well as some things you might still need improvement in? It's also important to hear positive comments about yourself from your classmates and teacher. Answer the questions below and share them with your class.

Write a few things you've learned in the following areas:

- Having positive role models: _____

  _____

  _____

- Being relaxed and comfortable in school: _____

  _____

  _____

- Making friends: _____

  _____

- Being organized: _____

  _____

  _____

- Listening to and following directions: _____

  _____

  _____

- Managing my classroom attitude: _____

  _____

  _____

CHAPTER 6
MANAGING BEHAVIORS
IN AN INCLUSIVE CLASSROOM

Effective classroom discipline is both an art and a science. It is an art in that an effective disciplinarian must be flexible in response to changing human behavior while understanding the importance of limits and consistency. This amounts to creative thinking and awareness of the individual student's needs as well as the needs of the entire class. It is a science in that effective discipline incorporates knowledge that comes from observing a student's behaviors and experimenting with a variety of strategies and techniques to help the student adjust his or her behavior. The effective teacher is constantly evaluating how the teaching process can be improved.

In inclusive classrooms, as in most general education classes, students' behaviors can be managed through basic structuring of the classroom environment with fair rules, logical consequences, and consistent enforcement. The rules that support a well-managed inclusive classroom should not be exclusive of the rest of the school. It is many teachers' experience that the most effective discipline plans are applied consistently schoolwide, so that wherever the students go they encounter the same behavioral expectations and the same plan.

CHARACTERISTICS OF A WELL-MANAGED CLASSROOM

✔ All students are involved in the learning process.

✔ Students understand what is expected of them and are generally successful.

✔ There is relatively little disruption and off-task behavior.

✔ The climate of the classroom is work-oriented, but relaxed and enjoyable.

Involving Students in the Learning Process

Learning is an active process. Helping the inclusive student participate in the learning process takes the same skills as those needed for the general-needs student, but they may need to be implemented at increased intervals.

To increase the amount of time the student is involved in the learning process:

1. **Check for understanding of what is being taught by asking comprehension questions.**

Asking and responding to questions is one of the most important processes that takes place in a learning environment, although research has shown that in some classes it's possible for days and even weeks to go by with some students never sharing their thoughts and ideas verbally in class. These few guidelines can be helpful for increasing students' active participation and opportunity for high response:

- Call on low-achieving students with the same frequency as high-achievers.
- Ask more open-ended types of questions versus single-answer ones.
- Call on females with the same frequency as males.
- Give students time to process the question or to think before responding.
- Ask a high percentage of questions that require higher level, critical-thinking skills.
- Rephrase a question if it is not understood.
- Return to students who do not offer answers.

2. **Stop after ten minutes of instruction to allow students to help each other clarify information being taught.**

3. **Constantly monitor students so as to keep them involved and on task.**

4. **Adapt or modify work so as to avoid frustration and/or passivity.**

Developing Clear Student Expectations

Class assignments as well as expected classroom behaviors should be stated simply and clearly to avoid any confusion or misunderstanding among all students. Here are examples of typical class assignments or objectives stated in clear and easy-to-understand terms:

✔ Name the three primary colors.

✔ Write three things you learned about reptiles.

✔ Create a new ending for the story.

✔ Share one important study skill you learned today with your learning partner.

✔ Plan a popcorn party.

✔ Predict what will happen next.

✔ Write a paragraph describing what you just read.

Some students with special learning needs, as well as others who are not necessarily below average, may need additional directions in order to complete the task and, therefore, keep actively involved. Accompanying the objectives can be specific questions that need answers. Next to each question a page number or location where the answer may be found can also be written.

Here are four examples of clearly stated **general classroom behavioral rules** that are positively stated, posted, and should be referred to frequently.

> 1. **Do your best, don't settle for less.**
> 2. **Respect each other.**
> 3. **Work cooperatively with others.**
> 4. **Stay on task at your seat.**

For some students needing very precise expectations as well as for the newer teacher, specific classroom rules might be more effective. Here are five examples of specific classroom rules that can be considered for creating a well-managed classroom:

> 1. **Follow directions the first time they are given.**
> 2. **Keep all hands, feet, and objects to yourself.**
> 3. **Change tasks quickly and quietly.**
> 4. **Raise your hand to ask a question.**
> 5. **No cursing or teasing.**

Keeping Students on Task with Little Disruption

Children want to know what is expected of them. High expectation is directly related to attitude and behavior. It is this behavior that supports high self-esteem, good grades, and, consequently, a successful school experience. The following procedures can help implement this aspect of a well-managed classroom.

1. The classroom rules and expectations are clearly posted and consistently followed. The rules can be given to the students in a handout as well or copied by students into their notebook.

2. Fair consequences and rewards are established along with the rules.

3. Posted rules are limited to no more than five. People find it easier to remember numbers in groups of three to five.

4. When a rule is broken, consequences are given with little discussion and with as minimal class disruption as possible. It is unnecessary to explain to a student why he or she must stop talking when you're trying to teach, beyond saying "you are distracting others who are trying to listen."

Do not stop the lecture, discussion, or movie. At times it might be more effective to wait until a time when the student is better able to accept the consequence—as long as the rule is not being continuously broken. You can go to the chalkboard and write the student's name or put a check next to it. At the end of the period, the student might need a "reminder" as to what the consequence is.

Establishing Consequences and Rewards

Rules, especially with children, must have consequences to enforce them and rewards to confirm them. Students will test rules to find the limits of their behavior and to find out whether the rule will be enforced or not. It is as important to post your expectations or rules, as it is important to post your consequences.

Most teachers at all grade levels use some kind of gradual step system of consequences for classroom management. Although the specific steps and consequences vary, the consequences become stronger as the offense is repeated. Here are examples of consequences from typical elementary and middle-school classrooms.

From *The Inclusive Classroom.* Copyright © 1999 Good Year Books.

Example 1

1. **Verbal warning**

2. **Time-out (5 to 10 minutes at time-out desk)**

3. **Time away in another cooperating classroom (also at their time-out desk)**

4. **Detention/vice principal/home called**

Example 2

1. **Verbal or nonverbal warning (pause, stare, pointed finger, etc.)**

2. **Student's name on board = 10 minutes of lunch detention**

3. **One check next to student's name = 20 minutes of lunch detention**

4. **Two checks = entire lunch detention, call home, and sent to the office**

It is important to note that these are examples of consequences and are not to be used universally. Lunch hour detention may not work or be acceptable in your school. For some children, sitting with the teacher at lunch may actually be rewarding.

Important Principle

Stating acceptable classroom rules should tell the student clearly:

a)   what constitutes acceptable behavior; and

b)   what are the consequences or rewards for the unacceptable or acceptable behaviors.

Using Logical Consequences

When consequences are not logical and do not reflect reason, they tend to anger not educate children. When children are angry they rebel. If a consequence does not follow logically from the behavior and instead is seen as arbitrarily imposed, the student will develop more resistance and ultimately defiance. The most well-intentioned teacher will become frustrated and most likely lose objectivity when dealing with the student's misbehaviors.

The effective use of logical consequences teaches students to choose between acceptable and unacceptable behaviors. They allow the student to experience the consequences of his or her misbehavior. Thinking of efficient logical consequences does not always come easily and can take some planning. Here are a few examples of logical and illogical consequences:

Student Behavior	Logical Consequence	Illogical Consequence
Passes paper in incorrectly	Passes the paper in again	Teacher throws paper away
Knocks over chair out of anger	Picks up chair and arranges all chairs at lunch time	Loses recess time
Walks in noisily	Walks in again	Teacher ignores noise
Does not write down assignment	Suffers consequences of not handing in assignment	Teacher deducts 10 points
Turns in sloppy paper	Does paper again	Teacher refuses paper
Throws food at lunch	Cleans floor in cafeteria or sits alone next lunch period	Loses recess time

Children learn better from what they tell themselves than from what we tell them. Using logical consequences takes the focus off the outside authority and puts it where it belongs, back on the student. Children may do what we order them to do, but their motivation to change a behavior must ultimately come from a voice other than ours—their own. They're more inclined to believe something that comes from inside their own heads. Logical consequences act as catalysts for thinking versus rebelling; "If I forget my textbook, the teacher will not give me another book, and I'll just sit there feeling bored," or "If I walk into class making a lot of noise, I'll just have to leave and walk in the right way." It might not always be possible or practical to enforce a logical consequence in the classroom, but any imposed consequences should always (1) be enforceable, (2) fit the behavior, and (3) be administered with *professional empathy*.

Don't React—Respond

Often our solution to misbehavior in the classroom is to react to the behavior personally rather than respond to the problem professionally. *Professional empathy* is the ability to separate yourself from the student's problem. Controlling your emotional involvement will assist the power of the consequence to take its course. Here are examples of statements that can be used before getting angry or pulled into the student's problem:

- "Really? Well I know you, and I'm sure you'll figure out how to get that assignment in."

- "I know how much you wanted to go on that field trip. How are you going to handle it?"

- "I understand your concern, but as you know, the consequence is a call home to your parents. Hopefully we can all come up with something to help you."

When we make these types of comments, we don't put ourselves up against our students. We instead give them the message that we are on their side, and that side is learning from their mistakes.

Rewards and Positive Incentives: Catch Them Being Good

In addition to enforcing consequences for misbehavior, teachers must give positive reinforcement for appropriate behavior. Many teachers have come to the realization that catching students doing what they should be doing and providing positive incentives, also referred to as positive reinforcement for appropriate behaviors, is the

most effective approach in managing the classroom. All students like and expect special recognition, rewards, or incentives when good work is being done or completed. This *proactive* approach towards classroom management is much more effective than being *reactive*. Effective teachers in inclusive classrooms spend time proactively, creating a responsive

> *"A positive incentive or reinforcer is something that follows a behavior, strengthening that behavior and making it more likely to occur again."*

classroom environment that prevents misbehaviors from arising rather than reactively dealing with problems after they arise. They do this by using positive incentives or positively reinforcing students who are acting appropriately *and* by making a conscious effort to catch children being good.

Studies have shown us that for every positive interaction in the classroom, there are four negative ones! That ratio at the least must be reversed. Taking this proactive approach can eliminate most of the discipline problems that occur in the average classroom.

When a positive incentive is used properly, it can increase students' desired classroom behavior. For example, a teacher gives an assignment and the students complete it quickly, quietly, and correctly. The teacher comments on how well they worked and gives them ten minutes free time at the end of the period or day. The following period or day the teacher gives them another assignment; they again complete the assignment quickly, quietly, and correctly. The behavior was correctly completing the assignment. It was followed by a desired stimulus or positive incentive, which was praise and free time. The result was that the behavior was repeated the following period or day. By catching the students doing the right thing with the addition of a positive incentive, the chances of them repeating the desired behavior were increased.

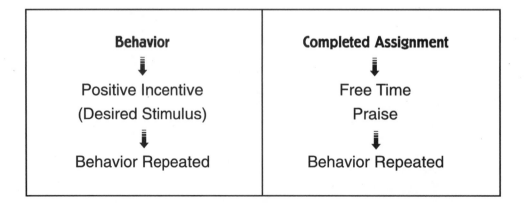

Behavior	Completed Assignment
⬇	⬇
Positive Incentive (Desired Stimulus)	Free Time Praise
⬇	⬇
Behavior Repeated	Behavior Repeated

This approach has again and again been proven to be more effective in keeping students on task than the "traditional" lecturing and punishing those who are off-task. If you find it difficult to find positive behaviors to catch, the student(s) is probably in need of modeling and direct teaching of what behaviors are acceptable. Expected classroom behaviors such as following directions and managing classroom attitude are directly taught in Chapter 5. There is an old adage, "Children learn what they're taught." This, of course, applies to appropriate social behaviors and social skills in a classroom environment.

Different Strokes for Different Folks

Not all positive incentives or reinforcers work the same for all students. It is important to know your students—their personalities, learning styles, and likes and dislikes or reinforcers. For example, having the teacher read one student's report aloud in front of the class would be very gratifying and, consequently, act as a positive incentive, but for another student it might be very embarrassing and could cause a negative reaction. Matching appropriate incentives to your students will take time and should be done with objectivity. A simple way of doing this is by watching students during their free time or asking them what they like.

A Lesson for Planning Positive Incentives

- **Activity**—Establishing Positive Incentives

- **Setting the Stage**—Ask students what positive incentives or rewards mean to them. What are their favorite incentives? When should they be given? Why?

- **Objectives**—The students will be able to:

    1. Identify personal positive incentives.

    2. Discuss when incentives should be given.

    3. Choose three to six incentives to be used in the class or personally.

- **Instruction**—Explain why this topic is important to you and that you feel it should be discussed in class so all students can participate in their own success in the classroom. Discuss the possible positive incentives for appropriate class behavior. Brainstorm and list on the chalkboard ideas for individual and group rewards. You can add your own ideas to the list. Have the students then choose three to six incentives for the classroom and/or for themselves. Post the classroom list and file the individual lists.

- **Guided Practice**—Present possible situations and ask students to discuss in pairs whether an incentive or reward is given. Return to the established reason for incentives and see if it supports their answers. Review your expectations with the class.

- **Independent Practice**—Ask the students to review what was discussed by discussing it in pairs and then sharing it with the class. Give the appropriate reward for participating students (i.e., stickers, certificate, note home).

There are three categories of positive incentives: *social, privileges*, and *tangible* incentives, or reinforcers. Social incentives are more readily available and usually reflect "real life." Examples of social incentives are the use of praise, encouragement, and smiles. The use of privileges can be a variety of potential positive incentives tailored to students' individual preferences. These would include free time, working with a friend, or having lunch with the teacher. Tangible incentives can be effective in some situations but should be the least used incentive and usually given intermittently or as a last resort when the others are not effective. They would include stickers, treats, toys, and tokens.

Research has shown that average to fast students seem to value privileges and nontangible incentives more than those students with learning difficulties. For the student with learning difficulties, tangibles can be effectively used in the initial learning stages but should be gradually phased out. Tangible incentives can also be traded in at the end of the day or week for privileges. For example, a fourth-grade teacher would give out apple stickers and post them on the bulletin board, and at the end of the week would ask students to trade them in for a privilege such as extra computer time or no homework for a night. Tangible incentives should also always be coupled with a social incentive.

Positive Incentives.	
Social	• Verbally praise specific behaviors • A smile • A word of encouragement • A pat, handshake, or high five • Thumb up • A note home, "Catch Them Being Good" notes • A phone call home • Honor roll
Privileges	• Free time, center time • Extra recess • Field trip, class party • Extended lunch time • Extra computer time, music, art, or physical education • Choosing class activity, being a captain of a team • Passing out papers, stapling papers together • Erasing chalkboard, feeding the fish or animals, watering plants • Playing a game with a friend or teacher • Tutoring a younger child, giving a spelling test • Delivering papers to the office • "No homework pass" for the evening, or good for one assignment • Taking one problem off a test • Assisting the custodian
Tangibles	• Stickers, badges, ribbons • Treats (preferably healthful snacks such as popcorn, pretzels, etc.) • Raffle prizes, pizza party • Certificate • Grab bag (small toys, trinkets, pencils, erasers, etc.) • Badges, buttons, trophies • Coupon for class or school store

The Effective Use of Social Praise

Many students who are underachieving due to a learning disability or some other cause often have difficulty accepting direct praise. Their self-concept, or how they perceive themselves, can be as one who cannot succeed. For example, when praised for doing "good work," they often think, "The teacher must not be telling the truth,"

> *"The effective teacher is constantly evaluating how the teaching process can be improved."*

or "What am I doing that is so good?" Students who are exhibiting negative self-images and poor self-concept often have low expectations of success. For this reason it is important to use *descriptive praise,* or to describe what the "good work" is. Descriptive praise is being more specific and naming the appropriate behavior. For example: instead of saying "Nice work" you would say, "You're taking your time to look up the answers. Keep it up!" or "You've been working for ten minutes without getting out of your seat. Great!" or "You're all doing a great job of reading quietly. Keep up the good work." Praise the behavior and then encourage the student. They will consequently be more likely to repeat the good behavior.

Changing Behavior Cycles

A study of middle-school children indicated that 3 to 4 percent of the children who were underachievers could be labeled as "lazy" and needed some firm consequences or reminders to motivate them. But what about the other 96 percent of the children who are underachieving? Their issue was not one of motivation but of self-image and self-esteem. Behavior is greatly affected by self-image, or how one sees oneself, and self-esteem, or how one feels about oneself. Children tend to behave in class according to how they see themselves and how they feel about who they are in relationship to others. The behavior in turn will usually validate the child's self-view that they already have. This creates cycles of "reinforcing attitudes and behaviors." Depending on the child's self-view, the cycles can be either negative or positive. Understanding the reasons for misbehavior and catching students achieving the smallest success in their behavior and attitude is often thestrategy that can begin to change a negative cycle into a positive one. (See "How to Change Ten Negative Behavior Cycles," Chapter 7.) Following are examples of what these cycles can look like.

Negative Behavior Cycle

Chris was in a self-contained classroom for behavioral problems. By the time he was put into an inclusive class, he had been told many times that he was disruptive to the class and disagreeable with his peers and teachers. He thought of himself as the child who always caused trouble. He thought of a lot of ways he could disrupt the class; after all, that was his distinction. He teased the girls, he hid other students' book bags, he poured plaster of Paris in the art room sink. Each of these mischievous acts and others like them brought Chris the desired result—he preserved his self-image as the "class troublemaker." Chris was so desperate for attention that he was also willing to receive the inevitable painful consequences. He acted in ways to confirm his negative self-image. This negative behavior cycle would likely continue for the rest of the school year unless someone could help change it.

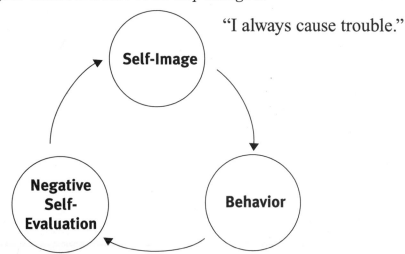

"I always cause trouble."

Self-Image

Behavior

Negative Self-Evaluation

"See, I've done it again. I'm the class trouble maker."

Teases classmates, disrupts the class.

Positive Behavior Cycle

Sholanda saw herself as popular, pretty, and capable. When given an assignment she approached it with enthusiasm, confident in her abilities. Her teachers and peers often expressed how responsible and well-liked she was. Because of her capabilities and dependability, she was often asked to participate in special projects and activities that increased her opportunities to learn and experience success. She acted in ways to confirm her positive self-image and, consequently, strengthened a positive behavior cycle.

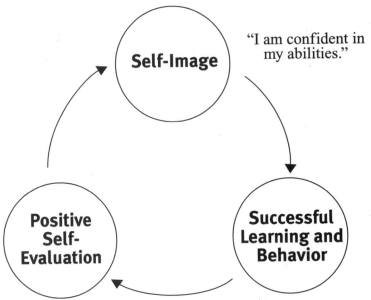

Self-Image

"I am confident in my abilities."

Successful Learning and Behavior

Participates in special projects and activities resulting in successful experiences.

Positive Self-Evaluation

"I had successful experiences, I'm even more confident in my abilities to do well."

How Does Self-Esteem Affect Learning?

Research about self-esteem and academic performance shows a strong reciprocal relationship between self-esteem and the ability to learn. High self-esteem promotes confidence and responsible behavior, as well as learning. In the inclusive classroom, teachers can be a significant link in helping all students develop high self-esteem by understanding the importance of noticing patterns or cycles that undermine or enhance the students' positive feelings.

The student with an academic learning disability or physical or mental disability need to acquire something equally as important as the skills of reading, writing, and learning. They need to gain *self-knowledge*—knowledge that lets them understand why they behave in certain ways and what choices they have in changing their behaviors. Helping children change their negative behavior and attitude cycles as well as to continue positive ones is the first step in assisting them in gaining self-knowledge.

Changing old patterns, as in breaking old familiar habits, is not always easy. It is not uncommon for underachieving students to seem to have no real motivation, no drive, or no ambition to succeed. Instead they stick to the familiar, or that which they are comfortable with, which often includes being "learning avoidant." But remember the other 96 percent of underachievers. A teacher deals with a motivation problem differently than a self-image problem. Students will sometimes give excuses for why they can't do something. Whether it's "School is stupid," or "Someone might make fun of me," or "Why try? I can't do it right," these students have a number of reasons for their reluctance to break old negative patterns. Children benefit greatly from understanding that obstacles can be opportunities. Helping them recognize opportunities in their lives can begin in the classroom. "Steven, what did you learn from this uncomfortable experience?" or "I realize this was a big challenge for you. Was it worth it? Why?"

Effective teachers will have high expectations for all their students and strive to help them fulfill their potential. The student who enjoys high self-esteem learns more happily and easily than one who feels inadequate. Students with high self-esteem, regardless of their disabilities, tend to be more successful, since thought and feeling *precede* action, and therefore the student is already "set" with positive expectations. Successful performance then reinforces their good feelings; the cycle continues to support successful achievement.

The child who believes that he or she is inadequate and unable to learn will avoid challenging tasks and approach new learning with a sense of hopelessness. Their attitude is "So why try?" This failure cycle is well known in education and with the arrival of inclusion is becoming increasingly prevalent: the child who has had early failures in school will develop attitudes of "I can't do it, so why keep trying?" Consequently, the student will almost inevitably fail at whatever task they try half-heartedly, unless and until the cycle can be broken with a renewed sense of self-worth and ability. Following are examples of how self-esteem can affect a student's ability to learn.

Negative Attitude Cycle

Sarah had difficult early years in school; her family moved four times between second and fourth grades. At the end of fourth grade, her classmates were easily reading grade-level books, but Sarah had trouble reading at all. It was decided that she would benefit most from repeating fourth grade because of the inconsistency in her academic instruction. In the fourth grade she was put into the "low" reading group. She began to feel inadequate and helpless as a reader as she watched her peers progress. When it was her turn to read, she became very anxious and frustrated as she stumbled over words others seemed to have little or no problem with. Reading period became a very unpleasant experience as well as an embarrassing time for Sarah. Anxiety alone made it difficult for her to listen and follow along as well as to really try the various techniques her teacher proposed to her. By the fifth grade, Sarah saw herself as a "bad reader" and thought it was hopeless to try to catch up to her classmates.

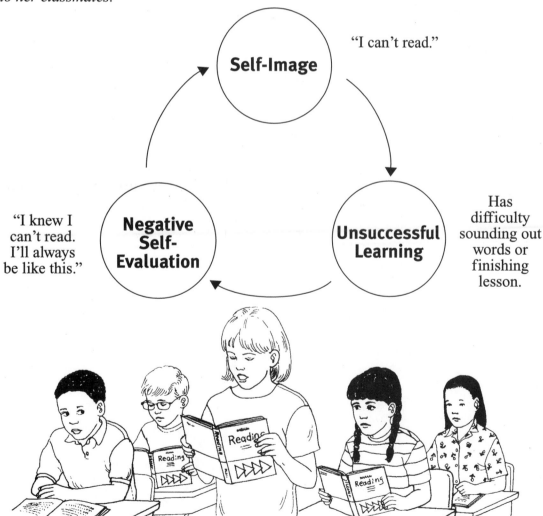

Self-Image

"I can't read."

Unsuccessful Learning

Has difficulty sounding out words or finishing lesson.

Negative Self-Evaluation

"I knew I can't read. I'll always be like this."

Positive Attitude Cycle

Luis was beginning fifth grade and was enthusiastically awaiting the first task the teacher would give. He was asked to be a "learning buddy" to a new student who needed help in math and reading. The role of a "learning buddy" required sensitivity to the problems and feelings of another classmate with learning differences, and the ability to help his buddy think through a problem and not give up so quickly. These are mature qualities that are not always demonstrated, even by adults. But his teacher believed Luis was capable of this task. He accepted the challenge, learned a great deal about others and their learning differences, and helped his learning buddy succeed with some otherwise difficult activities.

Self-Image

"I am able to help others and act responsibly."

Successful Behavior

Became a "learning buddy" and successfully helped with math and reading activities.

Positive Self-Evaluation

"I learned a lot and did a good job. I accepted a challenge and did well."

Self-Esteem in the Classroom

Self-Esteem Builders*

Students know what makes them feel successful or good about themselves. Here's what they say:

- **Smile when you see me.**

- **Call me by name.**

- **Listen to me when I talk.**

- **Let me know you missed me when I was absent.**

- **Recognize my own special talents, even if they do not show up on my report card.**

- **Give me a chance to succeed in at least one small way each day.**

- **Praise me when I do something right.**

- **If you do not like something I do, help me understand that you still like me as a person.**

- **Show me that I have a lot of options for the future, and that I can set my own goals.**

- **Encourage me to aim high.**

> *Try to reach each student with at least one of these self-esteem builders every day. They build stronger people and inclusive communities.*

* Used by permission of The National Association for Self-Esteem—Winter 1992.

Creating a Work-Oriented and Relaxed Classroom

Creating a work-oriented and relaxed environment is an important characteristic of a well-managed classroom. A majority of behavior problems can be avoided by establishing and then teaching students how to follow classroom procedures and routines. Children want to feel safe and secure in a predictable work environment. When asked, "Why was Ms. Johnson a good teacher?" one answer would always be, "Ms. Johnson made sure everyone worked together and she was fun!" Use the guidelines below to create a positive climate or "feeling tone" that will help students relax and enjoy the learning process.

Teach Classroom Procedures and Routines

Helping students understand how to stop talking or stop working and listen for instructions does not always happen when the teacher only tells students what to do. The students, especially those who are kinesthetic learners, need to experience an example of what should be done. This is why many teachers in an inclusive program fail when they want students to follow directions. The following three steps can act as guidelines for teaching classroom procedures and routines.

Step 1.
Explain the Procedure

First clearly explain the classroom procedure. Next model or demonstrate it. If the procedure has a few steps, demonstrate each one. For example, show how to put books away before lining up for lunch.

Step 2.
Rehearse the Procedure

After explaining and demonstrating the procedure, it is important to rehearse it until it becomes a routine. Children with emotional disabilities feel secure with clear and consistent routines. Having the students practice the procedure under the teacher's supervision, also referred to as "guided practice," gives them an opportunity to do it correctly. The procedure becomes a routine when performed automatically without teacher supervision.

Step 3.
Reinforce and Re-teach

After rehearsing the procedure, determine if all the students (or the individual learner you are teaching) have learned the procedure. If not, you may need to further explain, demonstrate, or practice what you are teaching. This process is called "re-teaching." When the students demonstrate that they can perform the new procedure, reinforce the learning with praise or a privilege.

From *The Inclusive Classroom.* Copyright © 1999 Good Year Books.

Following is an example of how a procedure can be taught. The important part of this lesson is the process of using the three steps–*explain, rehearse*, and *reinforce*–to teach the new procedure of how to quiet the class and have their attention.

A Lesson for Quieting the Class

- **Activity**—Procedure for quieting the class

- **Setting the Stage**—Ask students why is it important to be able to pay attention without a lot of noise and wasted time. Write the reasons on the chalkboard, adding some of your own.

- **Objectives**—The students will be able to:

    1. Identify reasons for quietly paying attention without wasted time.

    2. Follow visual or auditory signal to pay attention.

    3. Rehearse procedure until practice is not necessary.

- **Instruction**—Explain to the students that you have a procedure for when you want their full attention. Demonstrate how you will stand in front of the class with your hand raised. Also demonstrate how you might also hit a bell because some of the students may not be able to see your hand or hear a bell. Explain what you will expect the students to do after seeing and/or hearing the signal.

    1. Finish sentence then STOP talking and raise hand.

    2. Turn and face the teacher.

    3. Pay attention and wait for instructions.

    4. Repeat instructions and check for class understanding.

- **Guided Practice**—Rehearse the procedure by asking students to talk to a peer sitting next to them. After two minutes hold up your hand and/or hit the bell. Give instructions to have three students stand and share one part of their conversation. Repeat procedure.

- **Independent Practice**—When students can perform the procedure independently, then praise the correct behavior and encourage the students.

Teacher Alternatives

Behavioral Improvement Forms

At many schools, a variety of behavioral forms are being used to help describe the problem or situation the student is in trouble for and identify the appropriate way to deal with the problem if it reoccurs. Depending on the age and comprehension level of the student, these behavioral forms vary. The main purpose of using one of these problem identification and behavioral improvement forms is to assist the student in gaining ownership and awareness of the inappropriate behavior and then to begin finding a solution to the problem. Some forms simply have the child write what happened, who it happened with, and an alternative way of dealing with the situation if it were to occur again ("My Behavioral Improvement Plan," p. 133). There is a saying, "In order to change, you first must know where you are." Counselors understand that having children identify the problem from their perspective is helpful in taking the next step, which is looking at alternative ways to behave. (See the end of this chapter for other sample forms students can fill out.)

Using forms can act as a springboard for further discussion or create "cooling-off periods" before discussion. Younger children or those who have difficulty reading and writing, could have the directions read to them and/or draw rather than write about a situation. A child that chooses to draw can be asked, "Now tell me about the picture you drew." The child responds, "This is Jessica. She is drawing on my paper. I grabbed her pen and threw it. I was really mad at her!" At this point it's important to teach the child that their behavior wasn't appropriate, but that they also didn't make a fatal mistake. Giving the child an opportunity to talk with someone not directly involved with the situation that got him or her into trouble and then discussing with the child alternative behaviors can be very helpful and uplifting. It gives the child a way to start again and possibly see the opportunity in their mistake. It allows an objective person to listen without anger and judgment, and credits the child with personal responsibility for dealing with the problem.

The Behavioral Plan Form and Weekly Progress Report, pp. 134 and 135, are useful for communicating a student's academic and behavioral objectives and interventions with team members (teachers and parents).

Self-Monitoring Forms

The "Checking My Behavior" forms A (Middle School), p. 136, and B (Elementary School), p. 137, have been successfully used as a strategy for improving behavior in which the student controls his or her own planned intervention. The "How Do I Feel Chart," p. 138, is especially effective with helping younger children to chart their feelings and moods.

Self-monitoring strategies enable the students to reward themselves for a specific act. It is a method of shaping a student's behavior by gradually reinforcing the behaviors you want to change. It gives the student an opportunity to identify his or her *negative behavior cycles* and then begin to create new ones. By participating in their own behavior change program, children are more likely to understand their behaviors and the need to change. Self-monitoring empowers students. It also enables teachers to focus their attention in other areas.

Additional self-monitoring forms that can provide a nonpunitive method of assisting a student's personal behavioral management are the following: "My Classroom Rules," "My Classroom Consequences," "My Rewards and Consequences," and "How I Stayed Out of Trouble," pp. 139–142.

Researchers have reported high reliability for self-monitoring strategies. A general trend is that students are harder on themselves when judging their own behavior (Alberto and Troutman, 1986).

From *The Inclusive Classroom.* Copyright © 1999 Good Year Books.

Self-Monitoring Guidelines

- The self-monitoring forms in this book can be used as they are or as examples the teacher can adapt. (See the end of this chapter for sample forms students can fill out.)

- It's best to keep the list of behaviors to five or six.

- Be certain of the behaviors needing to be changed by observing the student for a few days.

- Include one or two behaviors that the student has or is close to performing. This will increase motivation and decrease fear of failure.

- Develop positive incentives, for example: "Three completed forms with four out of five behaviors performed correctly will get you. . . ."

- Since you are shaping behaviors, change behaviors to ensure success.

Alternatives to Suspension

In 1988 the U.S. Supreme Court ruled that students cannot be expelled from schools for behaviors that are directly related to their disabilities. For this reason special educators and administrators must set up alternative interventions for students who have persistent behavior problems. Pro-active behavior management can prevent most disciplinary problems from escalating, but suspension has also been a tool available to the administrator for behaviors such as fighting or destroying school property. Administrators who have students with behaviors that are more significant can consider these alternatives to school suspension:

- **Time-out:** Using extended time-out in another classroom, counseling office, or principal's office.

- **Loss of privileges:** Put on a "frozen list," which means loss of privileges for an extended period of time.

- **Detention:** Saturday detention (used at some schools with high success).

- **Parent/pupil day:** This is when a parent spends the day or part of the day with the student. This works especially well with children in upper elementary and middle schools. While the parent is in school, it is helpful to meet and formulate a behavioral plan at that time.

- **In-school suspension:** The advantage of this intervention is that it keeps the student in school, supervised, and still sends home the message of a formal suspension. For this intervention to be successful, the student needs to be given work to do independently during the day. Some schools add an additional day of suspension if the student does not complete the assignments.

- **Modified days:** This can be especially successful with younger children who find it very difficult to maintain a full day in school without getting into trouble. It is a temporary intervention that should be gradually increased to full-day participation.

- **Separate seating:** The student sits at a desk separate from the class, ideally with a partition between them. The student earns time back into the mainstream of the class as he or she earns points for completing work and following classroom rules. It is important that the special education teacher or instructional aide monitor the student's daily behavior. Check marks could be rewarded after every ten, twenty, or thirty minutes of on-task behavior. Some teachers have found using a self-monitoring form effective for this purpose.

- **School/community service:** It is not unusual in some schools to see a student picking up trash around the school building and doing certain reasonable jobs assigned by the custodian either during noninstructional time or after school. Other kinds of school service may include: cleaning up the cafeteria after lunch, washing the hallway walls, or putting away books in the library. (Remember that a consequence for one student can easily be a positive incentive for another).

- **Becoming a giver rather than a receiver:** Putting a student in a situation where he or she is expected to give assistance rather than receive it can be a catalyst for changing behavior. The student can be brought to a lower-grade classroom to help tutor younger children or children who are severely disabled. We have seen this intervention change students' negative behavior cycles into ones that result in rewarding mature behavior. This approach has proven to be more beneficial than punishments and negative attention.

Problem Solving

Problem solving is another alternative that makes the child responsible for finding an appropriate solution. A system in which students write problems and place them in a container such as a box can be used to facilitate discussion promoting problem solving. This gives the student a place to "temporarily put their problem" until it can be addressed. When time permits, the situation is either talked about with the children involved or with the class, and the class can decide on a consequence. In addition, the class can share suggestions for avoiding or dealing with such situations in the future. The teacher's role becomes a facilitator of respectful discussion and communication and the one responsible for handling those situations inappropriate for a class discussion format.

Steps for Problem Solving

1. Define the problem.

2. Make a list of possible solutions.

3. Look at the pros and cons of each solution.

4. Decide which solution is best.

5. Decide what has to happen for the solution to work.

6. Evaluate how well the solution solved the problem.

In the first step a clear and simple definition of the problem is decided upon and, if necessary, written on the chalkboard as a reminder. In the second step all possible solutions are offered. Then the solutions are considered, and one is selected. The problem-solving process ends with implementation and evaluation of the chosen alternative. This process can be used as a general classroom strategy for attacking any problem situation.

Introduce this method of problem solving by practicing on a problem that is not personal to any of the children. For example, start the discussion by saying, "Today I was almost late for school because I forgot where I had put my car keys. I'd like your help with finding a way to avoid this problem in the future. To help us work together, we'll use this problem-solving method (steps are written on the chalkboard and/or handed out to individual students). We then can have this method available to us for problems that arise in school. . . ." The "Steps Toward Solving a Problem" Activity Sheet, p. 143, can be a useful guide.

From *The Inclusive Classroom.* Copyright © 1999 Good Year Books.

Conflict Mediators

The Springfield School District implemented a peer mediation program that begins at the middle-school level. Teachers and counselors identify a number of students (both general and special education), who are then trained as student mediators. After they receive the training, the peer mediators are called on to handle some of the problems in peer relationships that occur among students at the school. Most of these conflicts revolve around such things as name calling, spreading rumors, and making threats, as well as general misunderstandings that lead to hurt feelings. In some schools, the mediation counselor coordinates the program and is also available throughout the day for conflict resolution issues.

Peer mediators are trained to ask questions such as, "How did that make you feel?" and encourage students to express to each other the effect the problem is having on them *personally*. Because students "speak" each other's language, it's often the case that they will more readily open up and express themselves candidly. The peer mediators help guide the process for reaching an agreement on the resolution, as well as putting the agreement in writing for the conflicting students to sign. Many have found that the mediation process has had a positive effect on solving discipline problems while encouraging students to be responsible.

School Counselors

Children with special needs can often benefit from developing a rapport with someone who can speak with and listen to them on a regular basis. School counselors are pro-active in providing support to students and staff, and can offer various types of services and strategies that are very helpful in inclusive schools. They can help problem solve, resolve conflicts, and act as an objective listener for students and staff. They also can teach lessons in self-esteem, social skills, and so on. The school counselor can be a support to parents and, when needed, act as a liaison between

parents and school. In addition to these support services, the school counselor can assist classroom teachers in setting up individualized behavior contracts, charting and monitoring classroom behaviors, and helping the team with other effective strategies and methods for improving behavior.

Instructional Aides

Often in the inclusive classroom the team includes a paraprofessional, or instructional aide. The special education teacher is usually the supervisor and direct supporter of the instructional aide. This additional adult is not only of great assistance with a student's instructional needs but behavioral needs as well. It is for this reason that students must be made aware of the paraprofessional's status, especially regarding discipline and classroom management. Instructional aides can work with both the regular and special education teacher. By law they cannot have sole responsibility for a student(s) with special needs or implement original instruction.

It is often the case that all that is needed to divert a behavior problem from escalating is another adult's support and attention. The paraprofessional can act as an extension of the teacher and be an invaluable resource for assisting with behavior management.

Helping Children with ADHD

What is ADHD?

Attention **D**eficit **H**yperactivity **D**isorder (ADHD), also referred to as Attention Deficit Disorder (ADD), is a complex and puzzling neurobiological disorder affecting many children in our schools, including many who also have learning disabilities. With increasing frequency, physicians and psychologists are labeling children as having ADHD. These children have difficulty staying on task, focusing attention, and completing their work. As one psychologist described this disorder, "For some children with ADHD it's not that they can't focus, but that they're focusing on too many stimuli at once." They are easily distracted, moving quickly from one idea or interest to another, and they may produce sloppy work that reflects their impulsive learning style. For these reasons, ADHD often interferes with a child's ability to function with success academically, behaviorally, and socially. Studies indicate that although ADHD, which affects approximately 3 to 6 percent of the population, is not synonymous with learning disabilities, up to 40 percent of children with learning disabilities display symptoms of ADHD.

According to researchers, there is a chemical imbalance in the part of the brain that controls impulses, aids in screening sensory input, and focuses attention. The causes of ADHD are not fully understood but are most frequently attributed to heredity, as it is found to run in families. As with learning disabilities, children with ADHD usually grow up to be adults with ADHD. Various prenatal factors, lead poisoning, and trauma at birth have also been identified as possible causes. There has been research that suggests diet, and more specifically the over-consumption of sugar and food additives, may be a factor associated with ADHD.

A very informative and well-written book on attention deficit disorder is authored by two physicians who treat children and adults with ADHD. The authors of *Driven to Distraction,* Dr. Ned Hallowell and Dr. John Ratey, have ADHD themselves and share some of their personal experiences of living with ADHD. One description they use is as follows: "People living with ADHD live in distraction and chaos all the time—bombarded by stimuli from every direction and unable to screen it out." According to these authors, medication that sometimes can be used in the treatment of ADHD "helps take the static out of the broadcast. It works like a pair of eyeglasses, helping the individual to focus."

Is There a Test for ADHD?

There are no objective and/or definitive tests (i.e., urine analyses, blood tests) to identify children with ADHD. *The Diagnostic and Statistical Manual of Mental Disorders* (DSM-IV) gives a diagnostic criteria for ADHD. Aside from this, a diagnosis is based on the following:

- Interviews with the parent and child by a physician or psychiatrist

- Questionnaires and rating scales filled out by the teachers, parents, and others working closely with the child

- Detailed health and developmental histories

- A thorough medical examination

- Work samples and any other testing results that may be appropriate

This information is then interpreted by professionals, who determine to what extent the symptoms prevail in different situations and evaluate other possible causes. Other possible causes that produce similar symptoms to ADHD include stress and anxiety in school and/or at home, learning problems, depression, and substance abuse.

What Is the Teacher's Role?

Classroom teachers must be careful in their role of "identifying" students who are suspected of having ADHD. The teacher's role is not one of diagnosing ADHD or telling parents, "You should see a doctor because your child probably has ADHD." The role of the teacher is to share objective information gathered through observations and personal concerns about their students with parents. Behavioral management strategies, classroom modifications, and any other intervention should be documented as to their effectiveness. Other team members, including the school nurse and psychologist, should be included in the communication process.

When a medical referral is made, the teacher(s) will be asked to fill out an ADHD Rating Scale. Sample questions on a rating scale can include the following:

Circle the number that best describes the child:

General Behavior	Not at all	Just a little	Pretty much	Very much
	0	1	2	3

1. Often fidgets or squirms in seat. 0–1–2–3
2. Is easily distracted. 0–1–2–3
3. Has difficulty playing quietly. 0–1–2–3
4. Often does not seem to listen. 0–1–2–3
5. Often engages in physically dangerous activities without considering consequences. 0–1–2–3

Inattention

1. Often fails to give close attention to detail. 0–1–2–3
2. Often does not follow through on instruction. 0–1–2–3
3. Often loses things necessary for tasks. 0–1–2–3
4. Is often easily distracted by extraneous stimuli. 0–1–2–3
5. Is often forgetful of daily activities. 0–1–2–3

Hyperactivity-Impulsivity

1. Often fidgets with hands or feet or squirms in seat. 0–1–2–3
2. Often runs about or climbs excessively in situations in which it is inappropriate. 0–1–2–3
3. Often talks excessively. 0–1–2–3
4. Is often "on the go" or often acts as if "driven by a motor." 0–1–2–3
5. Often blurts out answers before questions have been completed. 0–1–2–3

From *The Inclusive Classroom*. Copyright © 1999 Good Year Books.

Hyperactivity/impulsivity can sometimes be a component of attention deficit disorders. Young children at the elementary level with hyperactivity exhibit excessive gross motor activity, such as constantly running around or climbing. They are described as always on the go, "running like a motor," and having difficulty slowing down. They may not be able to sit for more than a few minutes at a time before beginning to wriggle around without stopping.

Older children at the middle-school level who are hyperactive may be extremely restless and fidgety. They are likely to talk excessively and may always be getting into arguments and fights with peers and siblings. It's difficult for them to keep their hands still while sitting at a desk; they may be tapping with a pencil, drawing, and so on. Giving these children something to hold and squeeze, such as a sponge ball, can be helpful and proactive in directing some of this hyperenergy.

Social Behaviors That Often Interfere with Positive Peer and Adult Interactions

Children with attention problems are more likely to suddenly change topics during conversations, fail to listen consistently when other children and/or adults are talking, and continuously look about the room rather than look directly at a peer or teacher. While these may seem like "innocent" behaviors, they often lead to other children or adults losing tolerance and avoiding interacting with the child.

Simply giving the student advice about more desirable social behavior (e.g., "You should look at people when they are talking to you, otherwise they won't want to be with you") seldom leads to changes of any significance. It is more effective for teachers to take an active role in designing opportunities in the classroom for the student to experience more successful peer/adult interactions. The following are examples of various classroom interventions for increasing positive peer/adult interactions:

1. *Catching them doing the right thing* and immediately using praise, a privilege, or a reward to increase their awareness of changing the negative behavior cycle

2. *Role-playing behaviors* that need improving (e.g., taking turns, sharing)

3. *Using peer models* for the student to observe and learn from. It's important to point out the positive social behaviors of the model to the child with ADHD in order to make them more notable.

4. *Designing special responsibilities* for the student to carry out in the presence of his or her peer group. This gives classmates the opportunity to observe the student in a positive light. For example, picking the student to be captain of a spelling bee team or erase the chalk board can enhance positive feelings between classmates.

5. *The use of medication therapy* to help some children with ADHD develop better peer/adult interactions by reducing aggressive, highly impulsive behaviors that interfere with successful classroom interactions.

Parents can also take a more active role, if they haven't already, in designing opportunities for their children with ADHD to experience more successful peer interactions. (See Chapter 8, "Teamwork with Parents.")

Children with ADHD and Their Positive Characteristics

Focusing on the desirable characteristics associated with children having ADHD will be helpful when directing the child toward successful learning in the inclusive classroom. Some of these characteristics include: being imaginative, innovative, interesting, and accepting; willing to take risks; having a boundless amount of energy; and being sensitive, observant, inquisitive, and good-natured.

How to Support Positive Characteristics

Supporting positive characteristics entails giving children with ADHD and learning disabilities what they need to be successful in the inclusive classroom. A list of these needs are as follows:

- ✔ Extra space
- ✔ Clear and predictable guidelines, expectations, and consequences
- ✔ Positive incentives
- ✔ Choices
- ✔ Adaptations and modifications of the environment and curriculum
- ✔ Multisensory instruction
- ✔ Ability to move around the classroom without disturbing others
- ✔ Extra time to process information and to perform tasks
- ✔ Modeling and teacher-guided instruction
- ✔ Reminders and prompting
- ✔ Help with coping skills and personal frustration
- ✔ An understanding and supportive classroom

My Behavioral Improvement Plan

Student's Name _____ Date _____

Directions: Put a check in the box after you answered the question.

☐ (1) What rule(s) did you break? _____

_____

_____

_____

☐ (2) How do you feel about what happened? Why?

_____

_____

_____

☐ (3) If something like this were to happen again, what would you
do differently?

"I would. . . ." _____

_____

_____

_____

_____

_____

_____

_____

_____

_____   _____
Student's Signature   Reviewed by (Teacher)

Behavior Plan Form

Student's Name _____ Date _____

Teacher/Room _____ Grade _____

To be monitored by _____

Behaviors that _____ need to be worked on:

1. _____

2. _____

3. _____

What does the student need to achieve to receive a reward? _____

_____

_____

_____

What will the reward(s) be? _____

_____

_____

_____

This Behavior Plan was given to:

_____   _____

_____   _____

(Parent[s])

Weekly Progress Report

Student's Name _____ Date: *From* _____ *To* _____

Grade _____ Class _____

Please review this progress report and any attached work *with your child*. After reviewing, please sign this report and have your child return it to school on Monday morning. Thank you for your support.

Behavior
- ☐ Good (G)
- ☐ Satisfactory (S)
- ☐ Unacceptable (U)

Work Habits
- ☐ Independent (I)
- ☐ Distracted (D)
- ☐ Unacceptable (U)

Is there work to be completed at home?   **Yes (attached)**   **No**

Comments from school: _____

_____

_____

_____

_____

Daily Record	Monday	Tuesday	Wednesday	Thursday	Friday
Homework					
Work Habits					
Behavior					

Comments from home:_____

_____

_____

_____

_____

Parent/Guardian Signature: _____

√ Checking My Behavior

Name: _____

Date: _____

Subject: _____

Circle *Yes* or *No* at the end of your class.

TODAY I . . .

Quietly walked into the classroom	Yes	No
Stayed in my seat during class	Yes	No
Participated in class activities	Yes	No
Followed the teacher's directions	Yes	No
Didn't distract anyone else	Yes	No
Filled out this sheet and got it signed	Yes	No

My ratio today is _____ out of _____.

_____

Teacher's Signature

√ Checking My Behavior

My Name Is: _____

Today's Date Is: _____

At the end of class read the sentences and then put a circle around *Yes* or *No*.

TODAY I . . .

Quietly walked into the classroom	Yes	No
Stayed in my seat	Yes	No
Did my work in class	Yes	No
Listened to my teacher	Yes	No
Did not fool around	Yes	No

How many times did you circle *Yes*? _____

How many times did you circle *No*? _____

_____

Teacher's Signature

Name _____ Date _____

From *The Inclusive Classroom.* Copyright © 1999 Good Year Books.

How Do I Feel Chart

Directions: Circle the number that shows how you feel. Then discuss with your teacher or a classmate: (1) Why you're feeling that way, and (2) What can you do to change that feeling, if you want to.

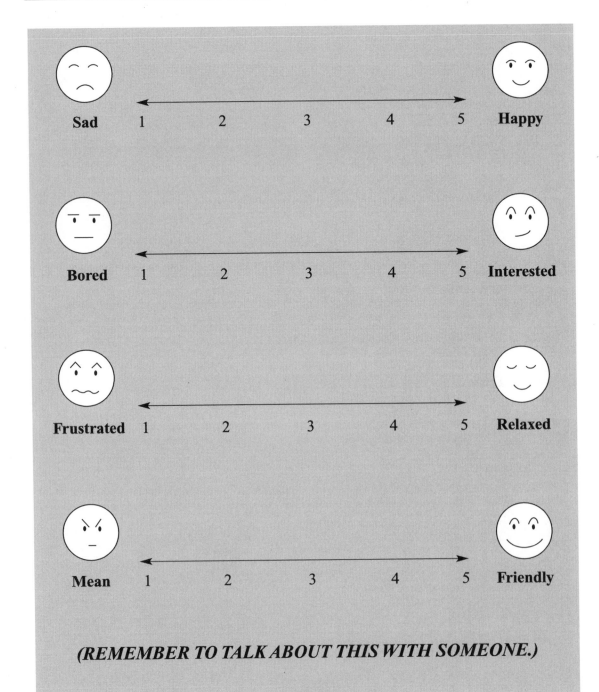

Sad   1   2   3   4   5   **Happy**

Bored   1   2   3   4   5   **Interested**

Frustrated   1   2   3   4   5   **Relaxed**

Mean   1   2   3   4   5   **Friendly**

(REMEMBER TO TALK ABOUT THIS WITH SOMEONE.)

Name _____ Date _____

My Classroom Rules

Directions: Write down the classroom rules that all students are expected to follow. After your teacher signs this paper, keep these rules in your notebook so you can read them during the year.

RULE #1 _____

_____

_____

RULE #2 _____

_____

_____

RULE #3 _____

_____

_____

RULE #4 _____

_____

_____

RULE #5 _____

_____

_____

_____

Teacher's Signature

My Classroom Consequences

Directions: Write down the classroom consequences to rules that have been broken. After your teacher signs this paper, keep these consequences in your notebook so you can read them during the year.

If I break Rule #1, the consequence will be _____

_____

_____

If I break Rule #2, the consequence will be _____

_____

_____

If I break Rule #3, the consequence will be _____

_____

_____

If I break Rule #4, the consequence will be _____

_____

_____

If I break Rule #5, the consequence will be _____

_____

_____

_____

Teacher's Signature

Name _____ Date _____

My Rewards and Consequences

Please make a list of the rewards and consequences of the class.

If I follow the rules of the class, I will earn:

1. _____

2. _____

3. _____

4. _____

If I break the rules of the class, my consequences will include:

1. _____

2. _____

3. _____

4. _____

_____
Parent's or Guardian's Signature

How I Stayed Out of Trouble

Directions: Write a short story or draw a picture describing a situation in which you used something you learned in class to keep you out of trouble with others.

_____

_____

_____

_____

_____

_____

_____

_____

_____

_____

_____

_____

_____

_____

_____

_____

_____

Name _____ Date _____

Steps Toward Solving a Problem

Directions: Fill in answers to the following questions. Continue on another sheet of paper if necessary.

1. What is the problem? (Pick a problem large or small that needs to be solved.)

_____

_____

_____

2. What are the alternatives? (List them.)

_____

_____

_____

3. Analyze the alternatives. (List best alternatives and tell why they are the best ones.)

_____

_____

_____

4. Decide. (Pick the best choice.)

_____

_____

_____

5. Evaluate the decision. (Did it work? Why? Why not?)

_____

_____

_____

_____

_____

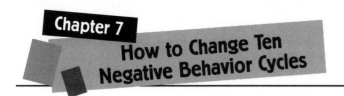

CHAPTER 7
HOW TO CHANGE TEN
NEGATIVE BEHAVIOR CYCLES

Negative behavior or attitude cycles tend to reinforce themselves, as shown in Chapter 6. For this reason when a student misbehaves, quick and immediate actions using correct discipline interventions are needed to interrupt the cycle. Unfortunately, what to do is not always so apparent. Studies have found that children with learning disabilities tend to attribute their failure to succeed academically and/or socially to reasons beyond their control. Therefore, they feel this failure cannot be changed.

Chris, for example, who was placed in an inclusive classroom, believed that he did not have the emotional ability to control himself and therefore was the "disruptive child." Sarah, the fifth grader, believed her mental ability would never improve and, therefore, she would always be "bad reader." In both cases, continued failure and helplessness tended to lower their self-esteem and reinforce the negative cycles.

To interrupt and change these negative cycles of reinforcing attitudes and behaviors, teachers are realizing the importance of individualizing behavior interventions, especially for the students exhibiting chronic and repetitive misbehaviors. The following examples can be used as a quick reference to ten negative attitude/behavior cycles that can be most often found in an inclusive classroom. Each intervention is divided into three reference sections.

Section 1. What is the behavior cycle?

This section describes a list of the specific attitudes and actions of the student. It is important not to fall into the trap of generalizing behaviors: "Oh he's just being a pain in the neck" or "She just wants to cause problems." Effective interventions begin with identifying the behavior. This will make it easier to describe the behavior to the student, team members, and parents, as well as identify the possible "self-message."

Section 2. What causes the misbehavior?

This section defines the possible primary causes of the misbehavior. Often we get overly involved with the student's actions and lose our professional objectivity and empathy when dealing with the problem. This section helps the teacher maintain a professional approach to changing negative behavior cycles to positive ones. This approach begins with discovering and then understanding the purpose of the misbehavior. Knowing the reasons why children act the way they do is the first step toward effective interventions.

Section 3. Interventions

This section suggests possible interventions to take to help the student change his or her behavior cycle. There may be several possible interventions or methods, and it is the teacher's responsibility to select the appropriate action that best fits the student's needs.

1. The Angry Student

• **What Is the Behavior Cycle?**

This student is always angry at something—himself, herself, peers, teachers, or parents. The student will become verbally and physically aggressive toward others even toward adults he/she doesn't know. *Self-message:* "I cannot control my aggression when I'm angry."

• **What Causes the Misbehavior?**

This student has low-self esteem and is trying to cover it up with angry-aggressive behavior. Low self-esteem can come from experiences in school and at home with failed academics and interpersonal relationships.

• **Interventions:**

1. It is important to respond and not react. Staying calm and not being aggressive in return gives the student little to fight against.

2. Listen to the student (when rational) and wait until he or she is finished talking. Ask if the student has anything further to say before you begin speaking. When you begin, speak slowly and quietly, modeling the correct behavior.

3. Communication is essential in creating a relationship with this student—so increase it. Arrange private conferences to avoid disruption and embarrassment. Do not lecture, but instead share your point of view on what has happened.

4. Explain clearly what sort of things need to be done to break the negative behavior cycle and make his or her behavior acceptable. Draw a picture of the negative and positive behavior cycles to demonstrate how they affect the student and others.

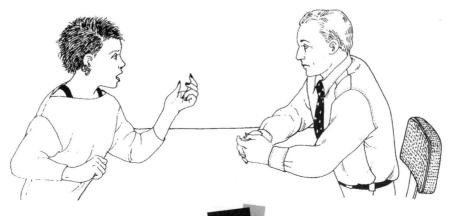

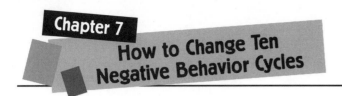

2. The Attention Seeker

• **What Is the Behavior Cycle?**

This student will usually be loud, speak out without permission, and act compulsively. He or she doesn't like being told what to do, but will do just about anything unusual to gain attention. *Self-message:* "I need to disrupt the class to be noticed."

• **What Causes the Misbehavior?**

The student who is always looking for attention wants his peers, teachers, and parents to know he or she exists. At the elementary level the goal is usually getting the attention of his or her teachers and peers. At the middle-school level, the focus may be one of trying to establish a relationship with the opposite sex.

• **Interventions:**

1. Meet privately with the student to give him or her an opportunity to discuss what might be the real problems the student is trying to solve by getting attention in inappropriate ways.

2. Discuss possible strategies you can use to help the student break this negative behavior cycle. These strategies can include completing a daily "Checking My Behavior" form, pp. 136–137, that can result in positive incentives and acknowledgment.

3. When speaking, model the correct behavior by not interrupting and by speaking softly.

4. Don't wait for this student to misbehave to get attention. Catch the student doing the right thing and use social praise as well as privileges. For example, a period with no inappropriate attention-getting behavior can be rewarded with extra free time with the teacher or classmates.

3. The Class Bully

• **What Is the Behavior Cycle?**

This student intimidates other students by verbally and/or physically pushing them around. He or she is always threatening to hurt someone and continually brags about their physical strength. The student avoids taking responsibility. *Self-message:* "I only get attention by pushing others around."

• **What Causes the Misbehavior?**

This student has learned that he or she can get the much desired attention of others by being a bully. He or she believes that being powerful or strong means pushing people around. This student might actually be fearful of others so instead will "beat them to the punch." Due to a lack of self-confidence, the student will usually avoid taking responsibility, such as accepting challenging tasks.

• **Interventions:**

1. Bullies need to develop a rapport with a mature, successful adult. This can be started by having short private talks or engaging in an appropriate activity together, such as playing basketball.

2. Speak and act gently but assertively to create a healthy comparison for him or her to observe. The Bully has the tough image perfected, but can't fight the gentleness, and that is what they really want.

3. Discuss their issue of needing to scare others to feel powerful and how it may act as a "disguise" for their insecurity. One teacher's method of pointing this out would be to make the analogy of the small caterpillar that has frightening-looking, hornlike hairs coming out from its body. The teacher asks the Bully, "Why do you think they have them? Right, to scare other creatures away. Do you think that's what you do when you make yourself big and scary to others? Well, I know why you do that. Like the caterpillar, you're actually feeling unsure of yourself and maybe a little scared inside. Do you want me to discuss this in front of other students, or would you rather we keep this between us?" Of course the answer will be to keep it private, but the important message is that the teacher now understands what is really going on and has shared this insight with the student. Change can now begin to take place.

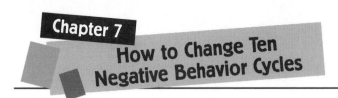
4. Emphasize the need to respect class rules and reiterate that disrespectful behavior will not be tolerated. State the consequences but always avoid putting down the Bully in public.

5. Consistently praise appropriate behavior and label the new behavior as being "strong" and "powerful."

6. A parent conference may increase your understanding of the possible causes for the child's bullying behavior. Ask other team members to participate in parent meetings.

4. The Swearer

• **What Is the Behavior Cycle?**

This student tries to impress classmates with offensive words. He or she has an appearance of being "streetwise" and a "know it all." The student tries to disturb others by cursing. *Self-message:* "If I stop using foul language, I'll stop getting attention."

• **What Causes the Misbehavior?**

This student is seeking attention and finds it by using profane language in school. When a student swears in front of the teacher, it can be disorienting as well as overwhelming for peers. It creates an image of toughness—that can feel powerful to a child. But in some cases it is a mere rite of passage, a phase children go through on their journey to maturity.

• **Interventions:**

1. When the child uses a curse word, pull the child aside and say, "I understand you like using those words, they do get people's attention—but they are not to be used in school." By saying this, you are taking the "air out of the balloon," which is the big scene that cursing may cause.

2. Ask the student if they will follow the rule. If the student responds with an "Okay," express your appreciation for his or her cooperation and that you'll let them know at the end of the day as to how they did. If the student says "No" to your request, respond with "Are you sure?" and wait for a change in his or her response.

3. To help change the negative behavior cycle, offer a few guidelines. If they respect someone they should always use respectful language when speaking to them and inform them that in most places, including school, swearing is not an acceptable form of communication. Teachers find that these types of suggestions are nonthreatening and will be readily accepted by students.

4. Offer substitute words such as "shoot" or "dang it" as replacements.

5. When foul language is used, never ignore it. Always interrupt and say something like, "Those words are unacceptable. I'm sure you can think of a more mature way to say that." It's important to increase students' awareness and self-control by insisting they "think" before they speak.

6. Reinforce the positive behavior with positive attention.

5. The Avoider

• **What Is the Behavioral Cycle?**

This student does everything he or she can to avoid working, such as sharpening pencils, needing to go to the bathroom, walking around the classroom, daydreaming, and so on. He or she can be disorganized and is usually unprepared. The student seems uncaring and apathetic, and avoids all challenges. *Self-message:* "I may not do as well as others, so I don't try."

• **What Causes the Misbehavior?**

This problem is not a lack of motivation but one of poor self-concept. Somewhere along the line this child was given the message that he or she was not measuring up to an adult's expectation, and consequently is filled with questions, misgivings, and lack of confidence.

- **Interventions:**

    1. Helping children see themselves differently by improving their self-concept will take time, but this is time well spent. Begin with acknowledging the feeling the student has of "I can't do it."

    2. Send messages that tell the student he or she has the skills needed to be successful in school. Each child must feel that he or she can keep up with other children in the classroom, on the ball field—anywhere children interact. You can't make a child successful. The child alone has the abilities to succeed. These skills are learned from modeling. Demonstrate how to begin a task. Pair the student up with a positive peer model or learning buddy. Good teacher models help students develop good attitudes and feelings about themselves.

    3. Create a written success plan for daily work goals. Give this student positive incentives for small successes and gradually expect more output. For example, after the student finishes one math problem say, "I can see that you are working hard to learn to do long division. Let me know if you would like some help, and keep up the good work."

    4. Confer with parents and team members. This helps the student to see the effort adults are making on his or her behalf.

    5. Develop modified classwork that matches the learning style and achievement level of the student.

6. The Excuse Maker

- **What Is the Behavior Cycle?**

This student often has a reason or alibi for not doing what he or she is supposed to do. The child can be very argumentative and often insists that he or she is right by rationalizing the inability to meet classroom expectations. *Self-message:* "I always have trouble getting my work done."

- **What Causes the Misbehavior?**

Using excuses and alibis to avoid work gives this student a reason for not attempting the work and failing. Discussion can revolve around the excuse rather than the cause of not making an effort. Poor self-concept creates avoidance responses that keep the child from dealing with their fear of failure.

- **Interventions:**

  1. Students who are constantly offering excuses or alibis may have lost interest in work needing to be done and/or feel it is too difficult to complete. Ask yourself if the work is too difficult for the student and whether a different or modified assignment would be a better match for this student's ability and interest. A sixth-grade science teacher trying to help a student who always had an excuse for not turning in his work noticed him looking at the eel in the classroom fish tank. The teacher asked the student if he was interested in doing a short report on freshwater eels for extra credit. When the student expressed interest in this project, the teacher worked with the special education teacher to help the child complete this report. When finished, the report was posted next to the fish tank with a large "A" at the top. This experience began a positive behavior cycle that continued as the teachers built on other small academic successes.

  2. Encourage personal responsibility. One teacher posted a sign in his classroom that read, "No Lies or Alibis." When a student wants to make an excuse for not doing something, direct awareness back to his or her own choices and possibilities in the situation. When a student says, "I lost my pencil," reply with "You can use this one, just sign out for it." If a student gives the excuse, "I lost my paper," respond with, "Do you want more time?" When alone, ask the student to discuss what might be the real cause behind the excuse.

  3. Avoid talking to the student only when he or she has a problem.

7. The Fidgeter

• **What Is the Behavior Cycle?**

This student is always on the move and cannot sit still for any length of time. He or she has a short attention span and usually needs directions repeated. He or she will ask to leave the room and is usually bothering other students. *Self-message:* "I can't sit still. I'm always disrupting the class because I move around a lot."

• **What Causes the Misbehavior?**

Do not assume this child can always control himself or herself. The causes might include hyperactivity, a symptom associated with attention deficit disorder (ADHD). If it is determined that the cause is a physical problem, the student might already be on medication. (See "Helping Children with ADHD," p. 128.) If not, then the cause probably revolves around the need for attention.

• **Interventions:**

1. After discovering the cause for the student's inability to sit still, begin to create a structured behavioral plan that assists the student's in-seat behavior. Have the student keep a chart of how many times he or she is instructed to sit down. Just bringing an awareness to this behavior will often decrease his or her getting up by at least 50 percent.

2. Create short-term goals for the student so that he or she can experience small successes.

3. Do not force the student to sit for long periods of time. Set a kitchen timer for successive ten-minute periods. Praise the student for each ten-minute period he or she remains seated. Gradually increase the time from ten to thirty minutes.

4. Give this student opportunities to move about the room in acceptable ways. For example, have them put away supplies, erase the chalkboard, deliver messages to other teachers. Establish a nonverbal cue that will give the child a signal when they can get up and move without disturbing classmates. Arrange class time for student movement into small and large groups.

5. Develop lessons that include activities for tactile-kinesthetic learners (e.g. role-play, performing, crafts, drawing).

6. Allow *any* child who has remained in his/her seat during a work period to play musical chairs, eraser tag, or some activity involving movement.

From *The Inclusive Classroom.* Copyright © 1999 Good Year Books.

8. The Teaser

• **What Is the Behavior Cycle?**

This student frequently teases other children. He or she makes comments at the expense of others, usually laughing at the cleverness of his or her remarks. *Self-message:* "I'm the class teaser and get attention for it." The attention is negative, "but at least it's attention."

• **What Causes the Misbehavior?**

In order to have high self-esteem, a child must have positive role models—role models that teach them how they should act, whom to respect, and personal responsibility. If a child is treated with ridicule, they will in turn tease others. This student is also seeking attention in a very negative way. After the negative cycle has been established, the teasing can become a form of defense from others "really getting to know who I am."

• **Interventions:**

1. Hold a private conference with this student and discuss the ramifications of teasing and why it needs to stop. Discuss respect and how such values result in behaviors that lead to success and reward. Develop an agreement that will give this child positive incentives for stopping his or her teasing of others. A "Checking My Behavior" form, pp. 136–137, can be used for self-monitoring.

2. Have the victim of the teasing tell the teaser how the teasing makes them feel and that they want it to stop. Pause, then have the victim say to the teaser, "Will you stop?" Wait for a clear response from the teaser. Let them know that you will meet with them again in a few days to see if the teasing has stopped.

3. Do not harshly reprimand the teased child for reacting. Instead, arrange with the child who is being teased that he or she will earn the privilege of helping you for a few minutes after school each time he or she is teased but does not react. The child can receive a certificate or "Medal of Bravery" for not reacting.

4. Avoid getting into the trap of teasing back. Remember the cause of the behavior and that ridiculing rather than counseling the teaser will only support the cycle of negative reinforcing behaviors.

9. The Property Destroyer

• **What Is the Behavior Cycle?**

The student destroys school and classmates' property. This student defaces walls and desks, marks pages in books, and repeatedly breaks things. *Self-message:* "I have to destroy things to get back at. . . ."

• **What Causes the Behavior?**

The student who repeatedly destroys property is acting out of anger and a need for revenge. Due to failure experiences, he or she feels the need to express himself or herself by acting out hostility toward people and property.

• **Interventions:**

1. Be certain the student who is suspected of destroying property admits to the incident. Otherwise, it's important to just discuss the situation without determining any consequence. Never ignore the situation; it will not just "go away."

2. Desks and walls that are defaced by pen or marker should be washed by the child to the satisfaction of the teacher.

3. Responsibility for destructive behavior must be taught to the student. With parental consent, if a student destroys another student's property, require him or her to replace it with an equivalent item.

10. The Chronic Absentee

• **What Is the Behavioral Cycle?**

This child misses school or classes for countless unacceptable reasons. Excuses that involve illness rarely are accompanied by a doctor's or parent's note. This child falls hopelessly behind in work and resists making up missed assignments. *Self-message:* "I can't deal with the discomfort of school."

- **What Causes the Misbehavior?**

This student avoids coming to school because of a feeling that he or she cannot succeed. There may be an unresolved problem concerning a teacher or classmate(s) that is causing the chronic absenteeism and need to escape.

- **Interventions:**

1. This negative attitude cycle is difficult to change unless the "past is dropped." When the student returns to school, the focus should be on the daily assignment and creating some successful feelings around being in school.

2. Failing to recognize and welcome the student in a genuine manner will only validate the child's negative image of school.

3. Communicate through daily interactions that you care about him or her and aren't going to give up on them.

4. Arrange for a parent conference to discuss possible causes and to develop an action plan that will include daily communication until the child's attendance improves. If the parents are uncooperative, it may be necessary to contact an outside social services agency that can provide supportive services for the child and family.

5. Watch for warning signs of potential problems *(proactive anticipation)* and *intervene* early. Award every child a star for each day's attendance at school. Have a perfect attendance party (include other classes) at the end of the week.

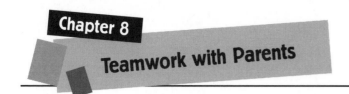
CHAPTER 8
TEAMWORK WITH PARENTS

Recent studies validate the importance of a parent's interest and involvement in his or her child's education. The research shows that schools where parents are involved had:

- **Increased positive behavior;**
- **Had higher test scores;**
- **Increased positive attitudes;**
- **Had more effective programs; and**
- **Had more effective schools.**

Children of all ages and abilities need their parents to take an active interest and place in the school community. For children who are experiencing difficulty academically and/or behaviorally, the first step in effectively addressing this issue is to increase the communication between home and school and establish a *partnership* for the benefit of the child. Students with learning disabilities and/or ADHD need increased supervision, monitoring, and reporting as compared to the average student. Input, involvement, and cooperation from parents will increase the successful placement of any child in an inclusive classroom.

Challenges and Concerns

The benefits are evident; therefore, what are the reasons that often impede the development of an effective partnership between parents and teachers? Some of the expressed concerns teachers have about parents and parents have about teachers include the following:

Teacher Concerns

1. A parent may criticize unjustly a teacher's ability to handle the class.
2. A parent may not trust the teacher's point of view and side with his or her child.
3. The parent's approach to handling discipline problems may be incongruent with the teacher's.
4. A parent may be a poor role model.
5. A parent may disrupt the classroom by being overly harsh with a child.
6. A parent may break confidentiality of the classroom by talking to other parents about another child's behavior.

7. A child may be embarrassed about having his or her parent in the classroom.

8. A parent may express interest in participating but doesn't follow through.

9. The teacher has little support from the administration for parent involvement.

10. A parent may become "overly involved" and not respect the teacher's position and responsibilities.

Parent Concerns

1. Parents may feel uncomfortable talking with teachers, let alone spending time in the classroom.

2. Parents may feel undermined by the teacher's authority.

3. Parents may feel intimidated by "jargon" and terminology the teacher uses.

4. Parents may feel inferior to the teacher because of his or her education.

5. Parents may not want to share too much of their home situation with the teacher and therefore the school.

6. Parents may feel the teacher is not sensitive to their child's needs.

7. Parents may fear the teacher is not really interested in their ideas.

8. Mothers may feel embarrassed if the child's father is not involved.

9. There may be a language barrier.

10. Parents may fear that the teacher will blame them for their child's misbehavior in school.

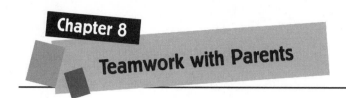
How to Increase Communication Between Home and School

Parents and teachers have their concerns and fears that go along with creating a closer partnership, but without parents' support and involvement, we as educators are very limited in how effectively we are able to teach our students. Therefore, we must open the door and greet each other in the spirit of facilitating an inclusive school.

The key to connecting school and home is *effective* communication. Effective communication can begin with a "Parent Welcome Letter" and/or "Parent Survey" (pp. 165–166). Establishing a positive dialogue with parents is the first step in effective communication. This dialogue can begin with a letter that welcomes the parents to the inclusive classroom. It can include some of your high expectations for the year and a request for parents' help in reaching and teaching their children. Helping parents support their children in the areas of doing homework, dealing with poor grades, and increasing self-esteem can be started by using the forms entitled "How to Help Children with Homework," "Talking to Your Child About Poor Grades," and "Five Steps Toward Improving a Child's Self-Esteem," at the end of this chapter.

What Else Can Teachers Do to Increase Parent Involvement?

Creating an atmosphere of acceptance in an inclusive classroom is also important for sustaining ongoing communication with parents. The following list of ideas that experienced teachers have used successfully are only useful if they are implemented. The time and energy involved in organizing parent conferences, school visits, sending home letters, and so on, will not happen without determination and effective planning. Organizing and letter writing are areas that a paraprofessional can assist with, as well as other team members.

✔ Schedule a weekly "Parent Guest Day" by inviting parents into the classroom to share their hobbies with the class (e.g., stamp or coin collections, painting, sewing, etc.).

✔ Schedule days when parents can spend a day at school by going to all their child's classes. Plan this for one parent at a time. "V.P.P."—Very **P**roud **P**arent buttons can also be given.

✔ Invite parents into the classroom to share information about their cultural customs, ethnic background, and/or religious holidays.

✔ Invite an interested parent to give you help writing a class newsletter. Information can include parent tips on helping with homework, responsibility, family fun, and so on.

✔ Invite parents to come into class and talk about their school experiences and what they would do the same as well as differently.

✔ Invite parents to assist one group of students with their assignment after you have worked with the students (e.g., the parents can reinforce a reading skill you've taught).

✔ Invite parents to work with a small group of children during a reading class. They can ask comprehension questions and help to keep them on task.

✔ Ask parents to be a one-to-one math, reading, or writing tutor.

✔ Have parents in the classroom as you teach a new skill. During guided and independent practice, ask the parent to monitor the work being done by students.

✔ Invite parents to chaperone on field trips.

✔ Invite the parent of the student who is being given an award, such as "Student of the Week," to share a few positive stories about the student to his or her classmates.

✔ Have a parent take pictures of the students and help create a display.

✔ Ask a parent to watch a particular television show with his or her child and discuss the show afterwards by filling out the "TV Questionnaire" form, p. 160.

✔ Send home weekly progress reports. Make a point of also calling and writing parents to share good information about their child's progress in school.

✔ Give parents small incentives for every participation effort, such as award certificates, **P**articipating **P**arent—"PP" badges, and so on.

TV Questionnaire

Directions: After watching a television show, answer the questions below.

Names of people filling out this questionnaire:

_____   _____

Date _____ TV program _____

What type of program did you watch (e.g., comedy, drama, documentary)?

_____

What was the TV show about? _____

_____

_____

_____

What was your favorite part? (Put initials next to your comment if more than one person is filling out this questionnaire.) _____

_____

_____

_____

Did you learn anything new watching this show? If yes, what? _____

_____

_____

Would you recommend this program to a friend? Why? _____

_____

_____

From *The Inclusive Classroom.* Copyright © 1999 Good Year Books.

From *The Inclusive Classroom*. Copyright © 1999 Good Year Books.

How Parents Can Help Their Child with ADHD

Teaching Children Social Skills

Parents can work on developing better social skills in their children. It's important to understand that social skill development can be a complex undertaking and that simply increasing positive social behaviors at home may not directly lead to significant improvements at school or in other settings. Nonetheless, it can only be helpful to make clear the social behaviors that are important for the child's successful peer relationships. The following are guidelines parents can follow at home to bring congruency with what the teacher is implementing at school.

1. Set up a home reward or positive incentive program that focuses on one or two social behaviors that need improving. These behaviors can include: taking turns, sharing, starting and maintaining a conversation (which includes listening), and resolving conflicts. *Catch the child doing the right thing*, and award him or her with a token. When the child has earned a specific number of points/tokens (for example, five), allow him or her to select a special privilege or tangible reward. Remember to praise the child immediately after the appropriate social behavior or interaction.

2. After observing the child's peer interactions, make a list of social skills missing from his or her repertoire. Use the following teaching strategies to work on developing positive social skills:

   • **Model**—Model the appropriate social behaviors by demonstrating the correct way to perform them. For example: Sit down on the floor with a partner and share a box of crayons while drawing together.

   • **Rehearse**—Have the child practice the behaviors.

   • **Role-play**—Role-play the correct behavior with the child. Then arrange opportunities for the child to practice the desired behaviors with one of his or her peers.

   • **Prompting**—Prompt the appropriate behaviors in social situations, either verbally ("Remember to share") or with some special signal.

   • **Reward**—Use praise. For example, "You're doing a great job of waiting until it's your turn to go." Include a tangible reward, such as a treat or grab bag, to reinforce the new behavior. Think of yourself as a "social skills coach" teaching new skills.

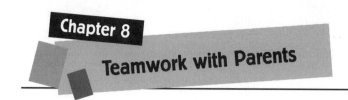
3. Videotaping can be a very powerful tool for change as well as fun to use together. While the child is engaging in an appropriate social behavior with a peer or sibling, videotape him or her. Then have the child watch himself or herself performing the correct behaviors. The child should watch the video at least once per day and before interacting with peers. This visual, concrete feedback can be especially useful for children with ADHD who lack self-awareness of their behaviors. It's important to note that videotaping inappropriate behaviors for the purpose of showing the child what he or she is doing wrong **is not** advisable. Children who lack self-control and awareness need to see themselves doing the correct thing.

Arranging Positive Peer Connections

The child with ADHD does not need to become popular in order to have satisfying peer relationships. The distinction between popularity and friendship is as follows: Popularity refers to how well someone is liked by the peer group as a whole. Friendship on the other hand, is when someone has a special peer to share positive interactions with. Many children with ADHD are not that popular with their peer group, and it's difficult to change their social status. A more reasonable goal for social interventions with children with attention deficit disorders is to establish regular positive contact with at least one other child after school and/or on the weekend. Positive connection with at least one other child can serve to buffer the child with ADHD from feeling isolated and rejected by the larger peer group. The following suggestions can be helpful for parents in their effort to arrange positive peer connections for their child with ADHD:

1. Encourage the child to invite a peer over to the house, and help arrange activities that are not highly interactive if the child has significant social skills problems. Activities can include watching a video and having a snack (e.g., popcorn) that both children enjoy. When renting a video, rent two and have the children come to a consensus as to which one they will watch. This sort of interaction is not highly interactive but can "build in" a positive and successful connection with another child.

2. Consider using short breaks from peer interactions, especially when things become excitable, or emotional. This would be time to "slow down" and reestablish better control.

3. Any signs of aggressive behavior should be redirected, because aggression is one of the strongest predictors of peer rejection with younger children.

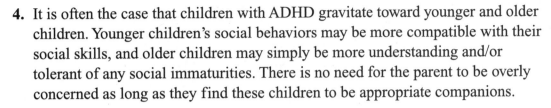
4. It is often the case that children with ADHD gravitate toward younger and older children. Younger children's social behaviors may be more compatible with their social skills, and older children may simply be more understanding and/or tolerant of any social immaturities. There is no need for the parent to be overly concerned as long as they find these children to be appropriate companions.

How Can School Help?

Peer interactions at home and at school can be quite different. School settings include:

a) larger groups of children;

b) different expectations for social behaviors; and

c) a more stressful environment for a child with ADHD.

Taking these factors into account, it's important that we consider the school setting when arranging for more successful interpersonal relationships for children with ADHD. Here are a few considerations the parent and school can consider:

1. Highly disruptive and inappropriate classroom behavior is strongly associated with peer rejection. It is important that parents and teachers work together to develop better classroom behaviors in the child. Home/school reports and behavior plans can be arranged for increased continuity and consistency.

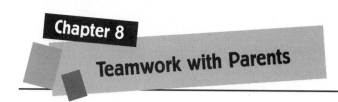

2. Parents should not be overly concerned about peer rejection if their child is receiving special classroom attention that results in other children disliking their child. Efforts should be made to change classmates' negative attitudes toward the child with ADHD by using a highly positive behavioral approach. Corrective disciplining measures should be carried out in as sensitive and private a manner as possible.

3. Ask the teacher to assign special responsibilities to the child with ADHD in the presence of his or her peers. This allows classmates the opportunity to observe the child in a positive light. The classroom teacher has the power and influence to change the atmosphere in the classroom from rejection to acceptance.

In summary, when parents are actively involved in helping their child with peer relationship problems, their understanding of the feelings and possible rejection associated with being a child with ADHD increases. The task is very difficult, and the parents should have realistic expectations of what they can and cannot accomplish. The parents' efforts in providing their child with opportunities for positive peer interactions and avoiding situations that can result in frequent social failure will hopefully create positive behavioral cycles.

Community Involvement

Across the country many schools are creating a truly inclusive education system that involves shared decision-making among various individuals of the school community. These individuals include: teachers, administrators (school principal), and parents. In some school districts, elections are held every two years to elect representatives who are responsible for making recommendations and decisions regarding curriculum, staffing, scheduling, community/parent involvement, and so on. Decisions are made on a consensual basis. This challenge creates a need for listening, respecting, and acknowledging all points of view. Schools that have empowered school-centered decision-making teams find that often faculty and community feel they have a voice in the important process of creating an inclusive school environment.

From *The Inclusive Classroom*. Copyright © 1999 Good Year Books.

Parent Welcome Letter

Dear Parents and Guardians,

Welcome to the beginning of a new year at _____.
This letter is written to let you know that your son/daughter is about
to begin a school year that will be filled with exciting challenges and
experiences. We are dedicated to creating a classroom environment
that meets the learning needs of all students.

We know our teaching must begin with making your child feel at home
in school and helping all the children come together in a learning
community. Please help us get to know your child better by answering
the following questions. Thank you for your time in sharing with us
your thoughts about your child, and we look forward to meeting
you soon.

Sincerely,

Your child's name _____

What are your child's strengths? _____

_____

_____

_____

What does your child need help with? _____

_____

_____

_____

Other comments _____

_____

_____

_____

Your name _____ Date _____
Telephone number _____ Best time to reach you _____

Parent Survey

Dear Parents and Guardians,

We would like your help in assisting us to become more familiar with your child. We are dedicated to meeting his/her academic, social, and behavioral needs. Please complete this survey about your child and his/her interests.

Your child's name _____

Nickname _____

Birthdate _____ Allergies _____

Your child's favorite things to do _____

_____

_____

_____

His/her least favorite things to do _____

_____

_____

_____

What are some ways you'd like to contribute to our class or school this year (for example, tutoring in class and/or on the computer, reading books, sharing cultural ideas, discussing your job and personal interests, etc.)? _____

_____

_____

_____

_____

_____

_____

_____

_____

Your name _____ Date _____

Telephone number _____ Best time to reach you _____

TIPS FOR PARENTS: How to Help Children with Homework

Dear Parents and Guardians,

Here are some tips for helping your children with their homework.

1. Create a game plan.

Make sure your child writes down all assignments in an assignment book. It's equally as important that they write down a word such as "none" if no assignment was given. Many children with learning disabilities could do better in school if they just got organized. They would get better grades if they did their homework on time. Classes would be more enjoyable if they brought in the right materials and completed special projects. Parents should plan to check assignments after completed. This will reduce missed assignments as well as offer children a feeling of accomplishment, a source of positive attention, and a connection between school and home.

2. Set up and stick to a homework schedule.

Deciding when to sit down to do homework can be a difficult decision for many children. Once the time is determined, it's important to stick to it as closely as possible. Supportive routines cultivate successful work habits that in turn help the child feel more confident in his or her ability to succeed.

3. Have a two-minute homework discussion before starting.

Discuss the different aspects of the homework assignment, such as what questions need to be answered before reading a chapter or how to study for a test. In this way he or she will have a clearer understanding of how to proceed with the work ahead.

4. Act as a resource not a helper.

If you act as a helper by sitting next to your child and making sure he or she understands the work being presented and making certain they complete it, the child will not likely learn to problem-solve independently. This strategy can create learned helplessness. Instead, parents serve their children better by being available for problem solving and clarification on aspects of the assignment given or by acting as a resource.

5. _Avoid completing assignments for your child._

If your child has difficulty completing the assignment and after honestly trying to do so, encourage the child to discuss it with the teacher. If you feel it is necessary, a note can be written asking the teacher to contact you if they need more information. This approach supports the child's ability to assertively communicate a problem and avoids the feelings of inadequacy that can occur if homework is completed for the child.

6. _Look for signs of learning problems._

Many symptoms of a more serious learning problem may show up during homework. Such symptoms may include taking hours to complete the homework; low frustration level; consistent complaining; and labored reading, writing, and spelling. If these symptoms present an ongoing pattern, a parent-teacher conference should be scheduled. One of two things will usually result from the conference, which the school psychologist and/or special education teacher should also attend. Either your child is having academic problems or is having difficulty with taking responsibility for his work, and the homework problems signal a need for better study and organizational skills. Neither problem means your child is a failure. However, by recognizing these homework problems and identifying their causes, you can work as a team with your child to solve them.

7. _Encourage good work habits._

Many children who have learning problems are not distinguished by their good work habits, cooperativeness, and productivity. To help this cycle of negative reinforcing behaviors, it is necessary to establish good work habits at home as well as in school. A simple method to support this goal is to use a lot of encouraging words when your child is demonstrating good work habits. For example, when your child sits and takes out homework, make sure you let him or her know you notice this positive behavior by saying something like: "Well, look at you, ready to go!" or "I'm happy you've started on your own." Continue catching the child doing the right thing with comments such as: "I'm proud of the way you are working" or "You're really improving."

Simply put, to change poor work habits to good ones, give your child _positive attention_ when they are showing you _positive work habits._

Sincerely,

Talking to Your Child About Poor Grades

Dear Parents and Guardians,

We understand no parent is very pleased to have his or her child bring home a report card with poor grades. However, the first thing a parent as well as a teacher should do is try to get to the bottom of why the grades are poor. Behavior problems that are caused by academic failure will usually disappear once the student gets additional help with academics. Academic failure caused by behavior problems, however, will not be solved by getting more academic help; in fact, the behavior can get worse and the grades will continue to stay poor.

Here are several suggestions for talking to your child about poor grades.

Don't

- *Scream at your child and tell them they are grounded for the next month. This will not be helpful in getting to know why your child got those poor grades.*

- *Lecture about how important school is and that they better "get their act together." This will usually put a child on the defensive and cause an argument or lack of communication altogether.*

- *Blame someone else for your child's poor grades (e.g., school, teachers, peers).*

Do

- *Talk and listen to your child. Let him or her know that you are quite concerned about him or her, but don't dwell on the report card grades (they can't be changed).*

- *Tell your child you want to work with him or her and the teacher to make school more successful. Let the child know you're on his or her side, and things will get better.*

- *Work out a definite plan for improving grades and write it out.*

- *Make an appointment to talk to your child's teacher(s). Bring in assignments that your child is having difficulty with. Work together to figure out why your child is getting poor grades, and then what can be done to help him/her succeed in school.*

- *If your child has special needs, make sure his or her special education teacher is at the meeting.*

Sincerely,

Tips For Parents

Five Steps Toward Improving a Child's Self-Esteem

Dear Parents or Guardians,

Below are five steps you can take to help improve your child's self esteem.

1. **_Support decision making and problem solving._**

   Allowing children to make decisions and teaching them effective ways to solve problems enhances their feelings of independence and personal control. Decisions about which clothing to wear, what friends to invite to a party, or what recreational sport they should participate in can give children a sense of control over what is happening to them. Children's natural tendency to exercise such controls can be supported or undermined by parents. As a child gets older, he or she should be given more opportunities to make decisions relating to his or her life. This preparation for adulthood will be invaluable.

2. **_Focus on solutions._**

   Someone once said, "There are no problems, only solutions." An important step in building self-esteem is to teach solutions rather than focusing on the problem or who's to blame. Children need to feel that they can influence what happens in their lives. To have such influence, they need to learn many skills. Teaching children the skill of finding solutions to problems or frustrating situations begins with statements such as, "Who's to blame is not important. The important question is, 'What can you do so this doesn't happen again?'"

3. **_Offer ways to solve problems._**

   Giving children options that they can use when difficult situations arise can enhance their sense of personal power. Offering alternative ways of handling an obstacle after asking children what they have tried enlarges their repertoire of possible responses.

4. <u>*Support responsibility.*</u>

Setting limits and rules adequately, such as requiring children to share in chores and duties in the home, are important factors in helping children learn to take responsibility. Learning to take responsibility is probably the most important ingredient in school success. Responsible children feel good about themselves, and they will want to repeat responsible behaviors.

5. <u>*Teach children proper labels for different feelings.*</u>

Help children identify their true feelings: "While the feeling you're expressing sounds like anger, it's really frustration, and frustration is. . . . Now that you know this, what do you think is causing . . . ?

Sincerely,

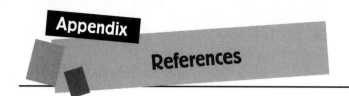

REFERENCES

Bauwens, J., J. Hourcade, and M. Friend. *Cooperative Teaching: A Model for General and Special Education Integration.* Remedial and Special Education, 1989.

Bos, C. S., and S. Vaughn. *Strategies for Teaching Students with Learning and Behavioral Problems*, 2nd ed. Allyn & Bacon, 1991.

Dishon, D., and P. O'Leary. *A Guidebook for Cooperative Learning: A Technique For Creating Effective Schools, 2nd ed.* Learning Publications, Inc., 1994.

Dunn, R., and Kenneth Dunn. *Teaching Students Through Their Individual Learning Styles: A Practical Approach.* Prentice Hall, 1989.

Gardner, H. *Multiple Intelligences: The Theory in Practice.* Basic Books, 1993.

Khalsa, S. *Group Exercises for Enhancing Social Skills & Self-Esteem.* Professional Resource Press, 1996.

Khalsa, S., and J. Levine. *Talking on Purpose: Practical Skill Development for Effective Communication.* Academic Communication Associates, 1993.

Lazear, D. *Seven Pathways of Learning—Teaching Students and Parents about Multiple Intelligences.* Zephyr Press, 1994.

Villa, R., and J. Thousand. *Creating an Inclusive School.* Alexandria, VA: ASCD, 1995.

ORGANIZATIONS

CH.A.D.D. – Children with Attention Deficit Disorders
499 NW 70th Ave., Suite 308
Plantation, FL 33317

Council for Exceptional Children
1920 Association Drive
Reston, VA 22091

National Center for Learning Disabilities (NCLD)
99 Park Ave.
New York, NY 10016

The National Association for Self-Esteem
1776 Lincoln Street, Suite 1012
Denver , CO 80203–1027

Inclusion Times
National Professional Resources, Inc.
25 South Regent Street
Port Chester, NY 10573

Parent Education and Assistance Program (PEAK)
6055 Lehman Dr., Suite 101
Colorado Springs, CO 80918

About the Author

SiriNam S. Khalsa, M.S.Ed, is a special education teacher, seminar leader, and author. He received a B.S. in Art Education and M.S.Ed from the State University of New York (SUNY) at New Paltz. In addition to his work as an Inclusion Special Educator in the Springfield, Massachussetts, schools, he also has responsibility as a teacher mentor. Khalsa has received special recognition from the Governor of Massachusetts, and in 1993 was honored as Special Education Teacher of the Year in that state. In addition to authoring this book, *The Inclusive Classroom,* he has authored *Group Exercises for Enhancing Self-Esteem 1 & 2* (Professional Resource Press, 1996, 1998), and co-authored *Talking on Purpose: Practical Skill Development for Effective Communication* (Academic Communication Associates, 1993).

The author presents a dynamic workshop on the topic of the inclusive classroom. If you are interested in sponsoring this workshop in your school district, please contact

SiriNam S. Khalsa
438 Long Plain Road
Leverett, MA 01054
(413) 548-9607